Producing Success
A Career Guide for Conference Producers

David M. Hoffman

Published by Gorilla River

Copyright © 2016 David M. Hoffman

All rights reserved. This book or any portion thereof may not be used in any manner whatsoever without the express written permission of the publisher except for the use of brief quotations in a book review.

Printed in the United States of America

Library of Congress Control Number: 2016908489

ISBN: 0692717315
ISBN-13: 978-0692717318

DEDICATION

This book is dedicated to thought leaders, innovators, and industry professionals throughout the land

CONTENTS

	Acknowledgements	i
Chapter 1	Welcome to the Asylum	3
Chapter 2	First Job? Some Business Basics	11
PART I	**SHOWBIZ**	**19**
Chapter 3	You Are the Emcee: Get Your Rap Down	21
Chapter 4	The Write Stuff: Your Journalism Pitch	31
Chapter 5	Everything in Moderation: Moderate a Panel	41
PART II	**YOUR NETWORK**	**45**
Chapter 6	Question Authority: Become an Authority on Asking Questions	47
Chapter 7	Enjoy Building Relationships	55
Chapter 8	Make Friends Who Spread Throughout the Professional World	63
PART III	**MASTER FOUNDATIONAL BUSINESS SKILLS**	**69**
Chapter 9	Project Management	71
Chapter 10	Put Wind in Your Sales	81
Chapter 11	Leave Your Mark as a Marketer	91

Chapter 12	Bone Up on Your Copy Editing Skills	101
Chapter 13	Become and Industry Expert: Go Buy/Sell Side	105
Chapter 14	Work Hard to Learn the Software	113
Chapter 15	Overwhelmed Yet? Get Used to It, and Learn How to Take Care of Yourself	119
Part IV	**THE GOOD LIFE**	127
Chapter 16	Travel: If You're Going to be There, You Might As Well Do That	129
Chapter 17	Find Your Inspiration	139
Chapter 18	Conference Schwag: Never Buy Another Pen	143
Part V	**JOIN THE 21st CENTURY STARTUP REVOLUTION**	149
Chapter 19	Learn the Intricacies of Working for a Startup	151
Chapter 20	Giving Back	157
Chapter 21	Start Your Own Company	163
Chapter 22	Conclusion	173
Appendix	The Producer Curriculum	177

ACKNOWLEDGMENTS

Special thanks to: Josh Kitlas, who convinced me that now was the time. Luis Benitez, the most talented designer in town. Lande Asiru, Brad Trechak, Percell Watson, and Jon Zelazny for editorial feedback. Todd Middlebrook, Lisa Weiner, Ethan Denkensohn, Bryon Main, Chris Skroupa, Andy Melvin, and Adam Raleigh for keeping me in the game for so long. And of course Alicia, Jackson, and Lily for inspiration and remaining supportive during missed weekends and late nights.

Chapter 1

WELCOME TO THE ASYLUM

"Control your own destiny, or someone else will." – Jack Welsh

Welcome to your new job.

You don't really know what you do for a living, do you?

Well, maybe you do, but nobody you know can describe it. Not even your boss and co-workers. You're sort of a writer, because you write agendas. Sort of a talent agent, because you book speakers for industry conferences. You may be accountable for sales in some way you can't quite control. Does interviewing a dozen people make you a market researcher? You may advise on what you'd like from the venue, but you don't get involved in contracting, so you're not a meeting planner. You're a producer. You do all those things, and more… and less.

If it's your first week, you're probably going to start second guessing this career choice [checks watch] about now. You haven't been trained very thoroughly, if at all. The company's stated expectations don't align with its incentives. The black hole of speaker acquisition has introduced you to an unprecedented level of anxiety and rejection. Your supervisor puts on a confident facade while he makes everything up as he goes along. You've caught a whiff of the scapegoating culture that permeates your company.

I've been doing this for more than ten years. I know that's shocking. I mean, there doesn't *seem* to be anything wrong with me, right? I'm smart, articulate, creative, always looking for ways to help. So why am I still doing this?

Because producing events fascinates me. It's about ideas. It brings people together. It's a strange corner of show business, a black sheep cousin of sales & marketing, and a rarely recognized sideshow of media. What's fascinating about the conference industry is that we build economic value out of nothing but the ideas and people we bring together.

It is hard work, but if you hit on a problem that really impacts an industry, you could conceivably build an entire event starting with nothing but the cost of a phone and internet connection - and make a nice profit while you're at it. You literally make money out of nothing but ideas. You deliver value by bringing the right people together. The relationships developed during the course of a single event can deliver an impact on people's lives, businesses, and the world.

"It's a strange corner of show business, a black sheep cousin of sales & marketing, and a rarely recognized sideshow of media."

I'm writing this book because there isn't much out there guiding you through your career. You can't major in it. Nobody knows what it is. You can spend twenty minutes explaining your job to your mother every Thanksgiving only to have her tell her friends you're a meeting planner. Most conference companies fail to provide adequate training for their producers, and the ones that do are narrowly focused on their own process and company needs. While companies that provide training should be applauded, remember that it is ultimately your career and life. In the 21st century, no job is likely to lead to retirement, much less in a high turnover industry like ours.

Throughout my career, I've visited three continents, talked to thousands of investors, innovators, and entrepreneurs, and generated millions of dollars with a product that you can't actually put your hands on.

I've seen a lot of good colleagues come and go, and a lot of frustration along the way.

It's true this job lacks structure, but understand: You get to experience things many people do not. Travel. Taking the stage to address elite audiences numbering in the hundreds or even thousands. Developing an extensive professional and personal network. Access to interesting and powerful people and direct conversations about their role in the world.

This book will help you if:

- **You want to identify mentors.** Each chapter points to a larger career niche where you can seek guidance.

- **You seek opportunities to improve and develop your job skills.** There are many opportunities on the job for you to practice valuable job skills. Additionally, the "Resources" section at the end of each chapter offers suggestions for further reading, training, or professional certifications.

- **You want to relate to the larger professional world.** You will learn the areas where your job functions overlap with the responsibilities of professionals in other fields, and where dedicating a little extra time can open new doors.

- **You hate the cynicism that is the trademark of our day.** This entire book requires an expansive, optimistic attitude towards work. The "Exercises" section at the end of each chapter will help you expand your outlook and improve your skill set.

- ~~**Your boss is an incompetent dick who is way over his head and likes to scapegoat.**~~ We know this one isn't true, because that would be cynical.

- **Your boss is a really nice guy who does his best and you want to improve your skill set so you can help him do his job better.** Your ability to help your boss achieve his goals is your biggest asset as an employee, regardless of where you work. The more you can give him credit for, the further you'll go.

- **You have a strong sense of agency.** Remember that nobody cares about your career but you. You may hear lip service, but ultimately, you're the only one with the vision of where you want your career to go.

You should always learn your company's expectations first, because being a good employee lays the groundwork for your work habits on future endeavors as well as your professional reputation. Beyond that, this is your career and you need to take control.

Define your own career

The lack of career development in this role is ironic. We're the ones who produce educational forums - often for continuing education credits - yet there is nothing for us.

Sadly, one consistent role I've played throughout my career is consoling or advising young, disillusioned co-workers. In his highly regarded business book *High Output Management*, former Intel CEO Andy Grove advises that training is one of the most high leverage activities that can be provided for employees, where investing a dozen hours in a training program leads to thousands of hours of increased productivity. You will be most successful if you view yourself as your own boss and seek out your own training. This book aims to spread hope across the ranks of my fellow ~~prisoners of war~~ brothers-in-arms that there are opportunities to build a robust career.

My goal is to use the territorial competition that often accompanies the producer role to increase the number of possible directions the job can open up for you. This is the 21st century and you don't need your company to define you - especially when you bring such a dynamic skill set. I'm all for business competition, and there are plenty of areas for an individual to find a niche for their own strengths and interests.

The bottom line is this: You have to invest in yourself first. Otherwise, you're a beer can your boss will crumple up and throw over his shoulder. Like the beer cans you may clean up on the side of the road when you're unemployed and looking for volunteer work to fill in the gap on your resume that will be there if you aren't proactive.

"This is the 21st century and you don't need your company to define you - especially when you bring such a dynamic skill set."

Investing in yourself means taking control of your career. If you view your job as nothing more than a way to make money, you will backslide if you become unemployed and have to dig into your savings. A few months without income can erase several years of hard work. If you rely on the confines of your job role for career development, your career will become stagnant if you go through a period of unemployment because you can't bring on the job training with you.

On the other hand, if your reason for working is to expand your skill set and you take control of this process by seeking educational opportunities outside of the parameters of your assigned job, your own value continues to grow as your work situation changes. The threat of unemployment becomes less daunting when you become proactive in your own career development. Ironically, unemployment also becomes less likely as you bring a wider mastery of skills and knowledge to the table.

This book will help you use your conference job as a lever for experience and growth while directing your own personal and career development. If nothing else, I hope it encourages you to develop the habit of looking for opportunities to expand your bag of tricks.

Join me as I give you a tour of this wondrous career of ours. Let's have fun.

CHAPTER ONE RESOURCES

Books:

- *Mastery*, Robert Greene

- *Mindset*, Carol Dweck

- *The Obstacle is the Way*, Ryan Holiday

- *High Output Management*, Andy Grove

Other:

- *Dilbert* cartoons. Read these for perspective. Work is weird. I guarantee you will see yourself, your boss, and your co-workers in these.

CHAPTER ONE EXERCISES

Describe what you do in one sentence. I like to say that I create economic value by leveraging industry relationships.
Come up with several examples that paint a different picture.

_____
_____
_____
_____
_____
_____
_____
_____
_____
_____
_____
_____
_____
_____
_____
_____
_____
_____
_____
_____
_____
_____
_____
_____
_____
_____
_____
_____
_____

Chapter Two

FIRST JOB? SOME BUSINESS BASICS

The first rule of being a great producer is to be a great employee. This is not that complicated. If you listened to your parents growing up, you should already have an idea on how to do that.

For example, one morning before my senior year of college, I quietly returned home after a late night out. I walked in the door and was surprised to find an angry patriarch waiting up for me. We stared at each other awkwardly for a moment before he launched into a brief, but stern tongue-lashing.

"Many managers say their greatest frustration is employees who show up tired on Monday because they were partying all weekend," he said, pausing to keep my attention. "By staying out all night drinking, you're putting yourself on the wrong side of that concern."

My father was mistaken. I hadn't been out drinking - what kind of lightweight is still awake at six a.m. after a night of drinking? I was, in fact, on the tail end of an acid trip. As such, what really stood out to me was the desperation behind his attempt at a strict sounding facade. He had obviously been up all night himself rehearsing this lecture. (If only more keynote speakers were as rehearsed as my father was!)

If your father isn't as vocal about his concerns as mine was (hopefully because you didn't stay out all night experimenting with an illegal synthetic mind altering substance,) you still have plenty of resources to learn about basic employer expectations. Seek out a mentor to give you feedback about your career efforts. Read industry books to learn from the experience of successful business leaders. Scan career related blogs such as LinkedIn Pulse, Forbes, or Business Insider, where every day members post their thoughts on the top five to seven ways to be a great employee.

Find a mentor

A great mentor can be a tremendous asset in planning a successful career path. If you're lucky, your direct supervisor will be a mentor. Even so, it's a good idea to find someone outside of your direct reporting loop to help you navigate whatever politics may exist within your company. This book will help you develop some career interests which will allow you to look outside of the industry for mentors. For example, a journalist's skill set involves cultivating sources. Someone who works for a news organization as a reporter or editor might offer an outside perspective on how you can build relationships with your friendly speakers and learn more about their current challenges.

> **"A great mentor can be a tremendous asset in planning a successful career path."**

To find a mentor, it's important to demonstrate that you have potential. A solid foundation of work habits and ethics will set you up for success anywhere.

Read books

Successful business leaders often write books to share their insights about professional success and trends in their industries. I always have one of these books in my rotation. I appreciate the little voice in my ear reminding me how to add value at work. I've worked at multiple companies that have official reading lists. Between you and me, managers love it when you show initiative by reading the books they suggest. If you read twenty of these books in a year you can synthesize a multitude of different approaches into the challenges you face at work. As a conference professional, I should not have to sell you on the value of absorbing a spectrum of experts' opinions!

Career blogs

LinkedIn, Fortune, Forbes, Inc, and Business Insider are just a small sampling of websites that allow bloggers to share their words of wisdom about how to achieve success. These blogs are repetitive, and can often be corny. But repetition is good. Adapting to a company culture is an acquired habit. The blogs are simply reminders to help keep you on track. If you need this advice, I suggest you take it!

Here are 11 of the "Top Five Secrets" that You May Learn from Blog Posts that Offer Career Advice

- Arrive early; stay a little later than required.
- Emulate your boss for cues on how to dress, speak, and behave.
- Follow news trends in your industry.
- Don't gossip; respect work boundaries.
- Always think in terms of "adding value" to your customers, your coworkers, and your employers.
- Do everything you can to make your boss look good.
- Treat everyone, including co-workers and external contacts, like your most important client.
- Finish tasks before heading home.
- Always use proper grammar and spelling (You spent tens of thousands of dollars on a college degree. Don't waste it because you didn't master a 4th grade English class.)
- Take care of yourself: get enough sleep, eat right, exercise, attend to loved ones, and so forth.
- Remember: Your career is your own. If you want to grow, you have to take initiative.

Pay attention

Ultimately, you're going to learn more by paying attention to the results of your behavior than from any other source. Self awareness is one of the most important predictors of career success, and you should learn to adjust your behavior until you get the results you want. This includes everything from your job role requirements to your relationship with coworkers. You will get further by learning how to listen than by trying to impress colleagues with your knowledge.

I don't want to digress from the focus of this book, which is how to make the most of being a conference producer. The point of this chapter is that these habits, and your reputation with regard to them, will follow you wherever you go, so get them down early.

CHAPTER TWO RESOURCES

Books:

- *Business Etiquette: 101 Ways to Conduct Business with Charm & Savvy*, Ann Marie Sabath

- *The Elements of Style*, William Strunk Jr. & EB White

- *Winning*, Jack Welch

- *The Rich Employee*, James Altucher

- *Swim With the Sharks Without Being Eaten Alive*, Harvey Mackay

- *The 10X Rule: The Only Difference Between Success and Failure*, Grant Cardone

Blog "Top 5" Lists:

- LinkedIn Pulse

- Forbes.com

- Inc.com

- businessinsider.com

Online Courses:

- iTunes University

- MIT OpenCourseware

- Udemy

- Corsera

Other Resources:

- Your boss

- An older co-worker

- An outside mentor

- Your Dad, Mom, older cousin, or crazy uncle – anyone in your family who has been around the block a few times.

CHAPTER TWO EXERCISES

Draw a diagram of your company's different departments.
Include reporting structures and demonstrate how they interact.

CHAPTER TWO EXERCISES (Continued)

Who are your major competitors?
What are five ways you can add value beyond your job description?
Who are five people you'd like to have as mentors?

Part I:

SHOWBIZ

So what professional category are conference companies part of anyway? I've seen many different descriptions:

- Think Tanks - because we create forums to discuss ideas.
- Media - because we bring content to audiences.
- Marketing - because we bring together buyers and sellers.
- Events - because they're events.

The job was first described to me as "Similar to newspaper reporting, but in 3D." I like that description because while reading a news article that synthesizes five expert opinions can be enlightening, hearing those experts engage in real time allows for a whole new dimension of understanding. As producers, we dig a little deeper into those interactions and direct the final presentation. It is a great place to be if you have a thirst for knowledge. We research and contextualize a story just like a journalist while enjoying the additional element of creating a live interactive experience.

The key driver of the following chapters is this: We're on stage.

Belonging on a stage is a privilege. It's an indicator that you're an important person who is worth paying attention to. People desire this kind of attention, and you are in a position to give it to them. In an age driven by "infotainment," being able to create a platform is gold.

If you haven't yet, you will soon encounter an unexpected problem on the day of an event. It could be a speaker no show, problems with the AV equipment, or, most likely, something nobody warned you about.

When this happens, you will realize the adage, "The show must go on" applies just as much to the conference biz as it does to show biz.

Chapter 3

YOU ARE THE EMCEE: GET YOUR RAP DOWN

"According to most studies, people's number one fear is public speaking. Number two is death. Death is number two. Does that sound right? This means to the average person, if you go to a funeral, you're better off in the casket than doing the eulogy." – Jerry Seinfeld

Speaking to a crowd of close to a thousand institutional investors and wealth managers at an event sponsored by Morningstar, MSCI, Goldman Sachs, S&P, NASDAQ and other leaders of the finance world at the Global Indexing & ETFs Conference at the JW Marriott Camelback Resort in Scottsdale, I made my first on-stage joke. "I was so excited about this event that I developed high blood pressure. So the doctor prescribed beta-blockers." ("beta" is another term for a market index, and beta blockers are a high blood pressure medicine. You'll have to trust me when I tell you that it is hilarious.)

Early in my career, I viewed opening remarks as an inconvenience. Speaking in front a crowd makes me nervous. In a room filled with hundreds or thousands of leading practitioners in various industries, I never felt like I had anything to add to the dialog. I was proud of my program, and wanted to run the show from behind the scenes and focus my energy on listening to the panels. I had recruited the speaking faculty and knew that they would say what there was to be said better than anyone. My remarks tended to short and factual. I just wanted to get on the stage and off as quickly and inconspicuously as possible.

I mentioned my minimalist approach to a colleague while preparing my opening remarks for an investment management event in Rome. My colleague was the kind of guy who loves the spotlight, and he reacted as though I had lost my mind.

"Dave, you've been working on this event for six months. I've watched you work your ass off putting this program together. You work ungodly hours. You put up with a ridiculous amount of bullshit from everyone around here," he told me. "Those people in that room at the Cavalieri Hotel are there because of all the work you've put into it. Those opening remarks are your reward. This is how you own it. You need to welcome those people to this event. You need to be gracious, enjoy that moment, and let that audience know how grateful you are that they can join you."

It changed my way of thinking, not only about opening remarks, but on conferences in general. It reminded me of the great value of the work that we do.

A neglected skill set - with hidden potential

While public speaking is an obvious complement to working in the conference business, it can also be a neglected skill set. It doesn't directly add to the revenue of the event, and people are really there to see your speakers and/or chairperson. The practical purpose for your opening remarks is to let the audience know the program is starting and to give them a few minutes to get back into the room. The content is generally housekeeping - reminding the audience when their first break is, or where the bathrooms are - things that are either in their conference materials, or are fairly obvious or easy to figure out.

But this is why the host role has hidden potential for skill development. The pressure isn't on you to perform. Corporate spokespeople, self-styled "thought leaders," and even stand-up comics would kill for the chance to get up in front of an audience of hundreds of entrepreneurs, investors, and C-suite professionals… especially the crowd of high-powered professionals and innovators you've brought together! We have nothing to sell. We are the host. All the pressure is on our speakers, not us. Developing your hosting skills is your opportunity to make the whole event more impactful for your constituents.

Six months before I debuted my sense of humor at the indexing conference I, shall we say, "beta tested" my comedy chops at a special open mic dubbed "The Heckler's Show." It was the most nerve-racking thing I had ever done. I was shy about talking in front of a crowd and this was an attempt to desensitize myself. The host encouraged audience members to try to knock performers off their game by heckling them; creating, in effect, a boot camp for aspiring comics. I learned the hard way that every line needs to earn its way into the routine because people's attention is a valuable commodity. An audience doesn't share their attention easily, and they don't take kindly to people who waste it.

I did a lot of research before attempting stand-up for the first time. In addition to listening to old George Carlin and Steven Wright routines, I read several books, and came across the idea that a successful stand-up comic could find a career as a professional emcee. A very successful one might find himself getting paid to host corporate events. I was encouraged when I read that because I realized that I was already a professional emcee who got paid to host corporate events. And so are you.

Being a great host/emcee adds ambiance to your event and creates a more enjoyable and memorable experience for everyone involved. Your opening remarks establish you as a point of contact and set the tone for the event.

As a professional, being a great host is an impressive, high-impact skill to have. For your company, you are in a position to make a standout impression on the minds of your company's patrons. Imbuing the event with a personal style makes it impossible for competitors to recreate the experience, even if they produce the exact same agenda. Not many of your colleagues will do this, so it gives you a competitive advantage.

Killer opening remarks

At the start of any event people tend to be guarded. As the day progresses, people loosen up and become a bit more familiar, making it easier for them to connect more intimately. A good emcee can bring this intimate atmosphere about more quickly because you have the ability to make the audience feel comfortable, starting with the opening remarks. You can set a tone of interactivity, humor, and self-disclosure that brings the onsite experience to the next level.

You don't have to be an industry expert, you just have to introduce the industry experts in an engaging manner. If you understand who your speakers are and why their background is important to the topic at hand, it should be fairly easy to command the authority you need to be an effective host.

> "Being a great host/emcee adds ambiance to your event and creates a more enjoyable and memorable experience for everyone involved."

You can do this by naming specific panelists or audience members and what they've accomplished so people recognize who is in the room with them. Asking a few preliminary questions of the audience also begins the thaw by getting the crowd used to engaging with the person on stage. Show of hands: Who traveled from where to get here? How many people work for universities? How many work for the public sector?

You can use these questions to demonstrate to your sponsors how many of their prospects are in the room and where they can find them. For example, if you are running a pharmaceutical research conference, you can ask, "Who here is looking to expand their clinical operations in the coming year?" This gets those audience members engaged by the simple act of raising their hands, shows them who else they may want to compare notes with, and allows any sponsors who can help them identify who they are. Since you have access to the attendee list ahead of time, you can calibrate your questions to make sure they elicit a healthy response.

Memorize to energize

Connecting with your audience starts with gestures. It is a primal part of how people connect because gesturing predates speech as a form of communication. Your opening remarks, by design, happen while people are just arriving, choosing their seats, and shuffling into the room. You are competing with the greatest amount of distractions of the day. You're the host, and it's your job to engage this audience. That's why it's incredibly helpful to memorize your opening remarks. It allows you to gesture naturally, and use this tool to attract people's attention. Eye contact becomes easier. If you're excited when you welcome people, you will naturally gesture. It's much better to allow this to happen naturally instead of standing stiffly behind a podium.

Remember: Your energy has a large effect on how people experience your event and perceive your company. If a speaker is a dud, follow up with some energy, ask for applause. As the host, you have the power to do this, and it is a valuable skill to develop.

You don't have to memorize much, and you don't have to memorize it right away. If you write your opening remarks the day you begin producing your conference and tweak them every day until the event runs you will have them memorized by the time you take the stage. They won't differ much from event to event, so memorization will become easier.

Put your stamp on it

The more of an impression you can make as a host, the more you yourself are branded as a differentiator for the event. Many of these events blur together in the minds of the people who attend them. (Surprisingly, changing the name of a *forum, conference, or summit* to a *symposium, congress, or meeting* doesn't make much of an impression in the minds of audience members.) Since they are attending events that address their professional niche, they hear similar topics and familiar speakers. If you offer an outstanding experience from the stage, you become a unique quality that people remember about the event. Not only does this give leverage to your company, it also brands you as a professional. You may be working somewhere else a year from now, and leaving a strong impression makes your job easier. The people watching you today may be in a position to recommend an emcee for their own corporate events in the future.

If you can master this skill, who knows where your career may lead? And if you think you can do better than my "beta-blockers" joke, get on stage and do it! (And tweet it to me at @forumplanner.)

An Outline for Opening Remarks

Half of the purpose of opening remarks is letting the audience know that the show is starting and it's time to filter in the room. But you can use the opportunity to warm up the crowd, and get them used to interacting with the person on stage.

- Welcome them to the location - make a joke or two, mention a landmark.
- Ask questions for a show of hands that highlights audience segments.
- Thank sponsors, speakers, and guests.
- Name on-site staff from your company - we're here to help you.
- Name the keynote and mention one or two of their accomplishments.
- Highlight a few sessions.
- Mention when the first break takes place.
- Remind people to ask questions and not be shy about approaching speakers to ask for more information.
- Suggest that the dialog doesn't end when the event ends, and that they should make plans to follow up.
- Introduce the first speaker/panel moderator.

CHAPTER THREE RESOURCES

Books:

- *You Are the Message: Getting What You Want by Being Who You Are*, Roger Ailes

- *Power Cues: The Subtle Science of Leading Groups, Persuading Others, and Maximizing Your Personal Impact*, Nick Morgan

- *Speak Without Fear*, Ivy Naistadt

- *The New Comedy Writing, Step by Step*, Gene Perret

Practice:

- Toastmasters International. www.toastmasters.org: Local groups that practice public speaking skills in a low pressure environment.

- Open mic comedy shows in your area.

Help Punching Up Your Opening Remarks:

- Fiverr.com: People will write jokes for you for 5 bucks.

- Upwork.com: Hire speechwriters with expertise on any topic.

CHAPTER THREE EXERCISES

Write a short opening remarks that applies to most of your events. Rewrite it one time every day until your next event. Rewriting it will take five minutes, and you will have it memorized in a few weeks.

Chapter 4

THE WRITE STUFF: YOUR JOURNALISM PITCH

"I became a journalist because I did not want to rely on newspapers for information." – Christopher Hitchens

A journalism background is a natural fit for someone looking to become a conference producer. And conferences are a great place to be if you're looking to become a journalist. Both require identifying and understanding trends, cultivating contacts, writing in a clear manner for an intended audience, meeting deadlines, and delusions of grandeur. "Conferences can be excellent places to access new stories and emerging research," Naveed Saleh says in *The Complete Guide to Article Writing*. "Conferences allow a journalist to interact with experts in the field and to network with other journalists."

Before I began my illustrious conference career, I was the editor of *The Hudson Current*, the arts and entertainment publication of the *Hudson Reporter* in Hoboken, New Jersey. I had absolutely no training in journalism before I got my first reporter gig. (Well, that's not 100% true. I had read thousands of news stories. Now that I think about it, I've also seen *2001: A Space Odyssey* a thousand times. Maybe when this conference thing runs its course, I'll get a job as an astronaut?)

It all began when I called the managing editor of the local weekly newspaper to ask for an informational interview. The editor asked me a few questions, and told me that they needed somebody to cover a town meeting that night. She offered me $50 to attend the meeting and write about it. I agreed, and that was the start of my writing career. My first freelance assignment led to a second, which led to a part-time job on the news desk of *The Bergen Record*. After several years covering a local New Jersey beat, I became an editor at *The Hudson Reporter*.

Before I made the leap into producing conferences, I got a job as head writer and producer of a Hoboken based TV show called *Across the Hudson*. Through celebrity interviews, live music performances, and visits to local clubs and other hotspots, we highlighted Hoboken's role as the fifth borough of Manhattan (Staten Island is the sixth. New Yorkers know I'm correct.)

I played a central role in that project and loved it. In addition to allowing me to interview iconic figures such as Artie Lange from the *Howard Stern Show*, Danny Federici from the E-Street Band, and Ken Daneyko from the New Jersey Devils, it added a new dimension to my previous experience as a reporter. In addition to seeking out stories, conducting research, interviewing people of interest, and writing, there was a third dimension of interactivity that came from watching my vision play out on screen.

After *Across the Hudson* ended, I got a phone call from a recruiter at a financial conference company who was looking for a producer. When he described the job as "newspaper reporting in 3D", I knew that I had found my new calling.

The purpose of this chapter is to help you reverse engineer a jump into journalism. I became a reporter with far fewer resources than you have as a conference producer. If reporters from Bloomberg and the New York Times look to industry conferences as lead sources, why not take advantage of your privileged position? At any rate, refining your research and writing skills while deepening your industry contacts will only make you a better producer.

Develop a love affair with the news

Every industry has trade magazines and websites that you should become familiar with during the course of the job. Your hook in getting industry leaders to speak with you is to write sessions which tie their job responsibilities into the most pressing issues facing their industry. The most relevant types of news stories are going to be business, economics, policy, and science. If you want to sync up with what your target audience is thinking about, you need to understand what problems they face, with an eye on solutions.

Read business focused news sources such as the Financial Times, Barron's, Wall Street Journal, and Fortune. In a way, everything goes back to finance because investors look at developments in their portfolio companies' fields. Set up Google alerts related to your conference topics all of your speaker's companies. Create a filing system where you save news stories relevant to your session topics. This will also help with marketing your event.

Learn sourcing and interviewing skills

The scope of your conference agenda is more expansive than a single news story, and your research doesn't get into as much depth. The depth of content comes out during dialog that happens during the conference itself.

"A journalism background is a natural fit for someone looking to become a conference producer."

The best way to get your sources talking is to get them excited about the topic, and this is best done with probing questions. Questions such as: What is the biggest change you saw over the last year? What is your biggest challenge on the horizon? How has this development affected your practice? and the favorite, What is keeping you up at night? will all get the wheels greased. The deeper you probe, the more textured your results will be.

During the course of producing an event, you naturally develop an army of sources within your industry. Your speakers and audience members are the ones who will give you a peek behind the curtain and tell you things you won't read in the papers. Successfully interviewing them requires you to research the topic ahead of time, make the subject feel comfortable, and let your questions progress based on the content of the interview itself. Your best source is someone who has the time and patience to explain their expertise to you, the layman. Develop a genuine interest in the topic, and your questions will naturally become more incisive. Remember to listen more than you speak.

Cultivate your sources - but protect them

Between speakers, sponsors, guests, and prospects you've spoken with during the production process, you have hundreds, if not thousands of contacts you can call up as potential sources for story ideas. And don't forget, you regularly attend events where the hot topics of the day are discussed.

As a producer, you definitely want to avoid anything that makes it harder for industry people to talk to you. Do not quote or source anyone who does not explicitly give you permission. I once wrote a marketing email blast highlighting four companies that were speaking on a panel. I immediately received an angry email from one of the company's speakers demanding to know what insider information I was sharing. Apparently, two of the companies had been planning a merger, and listing them in an email blast together raised a red flag at someone's compliance department. I was able to talk my way out of it, since I sincerely knew nothing about the merger, but the incident serves as a reminder to use caution.

What that means is that most of these sources are "off the record." "Off the record" can be an ambiguous term. You certainly cannot attribute a quote to an off the record source, but as a producer you don't need to use quotes anyway. Even if you could, many companies may resist speaking with you if you position your agenda research as an interview, as they may be required to go through a PR department for such interactions. Avoid going through

PR, marketing, or communications departments at all costs. You're looking for the real stories that will give your event credibility among your constituents.

Being a reporter is a full-time job, and you probably won't be able to interview your sources to the level of depth that the trade magazines you're reading require. The true value in your speaker relationships is that they can suggest what direction your should take your reporting or suggest story ideas to pitch to news outlets, even if they themselves remain off the record.

Write on the side

You don't have to start out writing about the topics of your forums. Write about whatever interests you. What you're doing is creating a side gig as a freelance writer on one hand, and cultivating your sources as a producer on the other. I do some side writing for aboutbluesmusic.com and bachelorvacations.com. If the time comes that you want to make a switch to become a full-time journalist, you will be able to demonstrate your writing with your side writing projects, and your research skills and industry relationships by referencing your event programs.

Conferences are deep news sources. You're at the center of all information that flows through the event. Not only do you get to listen to industry conversations during panel discussions, audience Q&A, and networking breaks, you're also sitting in on pre-conference panel calls where everything is discussed behind the scenes. It is good practice to integrate your notes into informative paragraphs and probing questions in order to deepen your understanding of the topic.

Learn how to write in a manner that is similar to the news stories you're reading. The first and easiest way to practice writing in a news style is to start a blog. You can use open platforms such as WordPress or Medium.com. As you adopt an authoritative tone, LinkedIn Pulse or SeekingAlpha offer more professional outlets. When you become comfortable, solicit publications on the side to write for. Become familiar with what news stories are being covered in the major news sources such as the CNBC or the Wall Street Journal. If you establish some sort of expertise, sites like Forbes.com have blogger columnists. The big news websites such as the New York Times, Washington Post, and Financial Times all use freelancers who have niche beats.

Get to know journalists

After producing several conferences, you will likely have dozens of connections within the journalism space, including reporters and editors at trade publications.

On the way back from a private equity event I launched in Madrid, I struck up a conversation with the person sitting next to me. It turned out that she was a reporter from Thompson Reuters who had interviewed speakers for a webcast at the 2014 Alpha Hedge East at the PGA Resort in Palm Beach Gardens, which I had run about two months earlier. We did not recognize each other, which was funny because we had been the two most visible people at the event, me running everything from the stage, and her interviewing most of the speakers outside, but our paths hadn't crossed.

"After producing several conferences, you will likely have dozens of connections within the journalism space."

Many events actively invite the press, and some companies encourage producers to use journalists as panel moderators. Journalists often make great panel moderators as interviewing people is their core competency and they are well versed in the topics being discussed. It is a best practice among sponsorship managers to introduce their clients to potential customers in the audience. You can follow their lead and deepen your relationships within the media by introducing your guests from the press to possible sources who are attending your event.

If you effectively cultivate a wealth of sources, topic knowledge, interviewing skills, writing ability and contacts within the news industry, you should be able to parlay your day job into side work as a writer or reporter, if not eventually move in that direction full-time.

CHAPTER FOUR RESOURCES

Books:

- *The Complete Reporter: Fundamentals of News Gathering, Writing, and Editing,* Leiter, Harriss & Johnson

- *The Associated Press Stylebook and Briefing on Media Law*

- *The Complete Guide to Article Writing,* Naveed Saleh

- *The Interviewer's Handbook: A Guerrilla Guide,* John Brady

- *The Art of the Interview: Lessons from a Master of the Craft,* Lawrence Grobel

Online Training:

- Poynter Institute. www.poynter.org: Has short classes and mini-certificates to help you develop various reporting and writing skills.

- Writer's Digest University www.writersonlineworkshops.com

Blog Platforms:

- Forbes.com

- Seekingalpha.com

- WordPress.com
- Medium.com

CHAPTER FOUR EXERCISES

Who are your top five sources? ("friendlies", in conference terms)
What are the top five issues in your industry today?
What are the tip five industry publications your audience reads?

Chapter 5

EVERYTHING IN MODERATION: MODERATE A PANEL

"There are no bad guests, only bad hosts." – Joe Franklin

If you have a few events under your belt, you have probably run a few pre-conference panel calls. When I prepped guests for my television show, this was called the pre-interview. I'd like to turn you on to the possibility of moderating a panel yourself.

Moderating a panel is a great way to hone your journalism and public speaking skills. As host you may have an opportunity to interview a keynote speaker, or fill in when a moderator can't make it.

Leading the conversation in front of a crowd is daunting, and that is why it is a unique, visible, and high profile skill to bring to the job market. When I contracted with the Conference Board, I produced and hosted webcasts on public-private partnerships, investing in sustainable businesses, and corporate driven recycling efforts.

Deep down, you may already be tempted to take the stage and moderate a panel. Allow yourself to enjoy it. I think you might find it to be irresistible.

Take advice from Joe Franklin

The best advice I can offer a new moderator was given to me by Joe Franklin, the television legend who invented the talk show format we emulate. He also had a radio show that was on the air for 40 years. I own the distinction of being the last person he introduced to his audience before signing off in 2004.

"What would you say is the key to a good interview?" I asked him, on the air.

Joe considered for a moment and then passed the question to the legendary mentalist The Amazing Kreskin, sitting two seats down from me.

"You do something nobody does anymore," said Kreskin. "Listen."

Indeed, the ability to listen—not only to your panelists, but to any questions from the audience—is a far greater asset for running an engaging panel than any level of industry knowledge or dramatic stage presence. It is probably the biggest asset you bring to the table as a producer.

Joe once told me there are no bad guests, only bad hosts. And he demonstrated this with a video reel of a local impressionist. The video was painful to watch. For an hour and a half I watched this poor fellow do impressions of Dr. Ruth and Ronald Reagan at birthday parties and Elks Club meetings. It was embarrassingly unfunny. The only reason I stuck with it was out of respect for Joe. Towards the end of the tape however, was a segment where this guy was a guest on the Joe Franklin show.

Suddenly, the guy was hilarious. Joe knew exactly how to squeeze some legitimately funny moments out of him. The panel had two other guests, who Joe interviewed as one would expect. But occasionally, Joe would ask this guy, "What do you think Dr. Ruth?"

or, "I think Ronald Reagan has something to say," and the guy hit the mark every time. It was really funny and a testament to Joe's entertainment sense.

As a moderator you put yourself in the center of high-level discussion about the topic. Your listening skills and ability to ask insightful questions allows people to look to you as a guide who will help them find the expertise they are looking for. Think about how to be compelling, and you will create an air of authority that will brand you as a leader in your field.

David M. Hoffman

PART II

YOUR NETWORK

Sometimes it feels like you bleed your soul dry building a business for your employer.

And I'm not going to lie to you. You are.

But the fact is, every hour of sweat you put into your job, you're also building up your own network. As a producer, you are an expert in creating economic value by providing a platform for people to leverage their competencies and introducing them to potential partners, customers, and mentors. Your network is a bit of leverage that can't be taken away from you.

Your boss can make you sign a non-compete contract stating that you will not build an identical event to ones you build for him, but he can't take away the relationships you form, nor dictate what you do in the future.

You are in a perfect position to network your way to anyone you can imagine. The next section discusses how to build a network that will help you realize your dreams.

David M. Hoffman

Chapter 6

QUESTION AUTHORITY: BECOME AN AUTHORITY IN ASKING QUESTIONS

"I remind myself every morning: Nothing I say this day will teach me anything. So if I'm going to learn, I must do it by listening." – Larry King

Have you ever put any thought into what questions you ask someone when you meet for the first time? Actually, forget that. That's a closed ended question. The only options are "yes" or "no." I should have said, How do you decide what questions you're going to ask someone when you meet them for the first time? That is a good starting point for this chapter.

Your relationships are made up of your personal connections and your network. But perhaps your best friends are questions themselves. In his classic self improvement book *Awaken the Giant Within*, Tony Robbins says the questions you ask yourself are so important they can determine the quality of your life.

"Questions set off a processional effect that has an impact beyond our imagination," Robbins says. "Questioning our limitations is what tears down the walls in life - in business, in relationships, between countries. *I believe all human progress is preceded by new questions."*

In the conference game, questions are the oil that lubricates both your research and your hosting duties. The key in both cases is to be genuinely curious, and interested in other people. An important principle in Dale Carnegie's *How to Win Friends and Influence People*, is "Become genuinely interested in other people."

"A show of interest, as with every other principle of human relations, must be sincere," Carnegie tells us. "It must not only pay off for the person showing the interest, but for the person receiving the attention. It is a two-way street - both parties benefit."

Questions are how you engage people and get them to open up. You're corralling hundreds of people through your production process. Outreach is hard. But if you actively engage people, they will come to you.

> **Some Questions you Can Ask When Talking to Guests Onsite**
>
> - How did you get started in this industry?
> - What is the best part about working in this position?
> - How is your industry different now than when you started?
> - What did you think of [a specific detail regarding the last panel]?
> - How is your company different from the competition?
> - Have you always worked in this vertical?
> - What are you hoping to learn at this event?
> - Which panel are you most looking forward to/did you enjoy the most?
> - What would you recommend I do tonight in this city?
> - Where are you traveling to next?

If engagement seems intimidating, remember: you are actually in a privileged position onsite in that nobody expects you to be interesting. In fact, the last thing they want is for you to distract the people they want to meet. So the best thing you can do when connecting with your speakers and guests is to get them talking about themselves.

By asking questions about their job and their trip, you are priming them to more effectively talk about others, as your questions can help them prepare to better present themselves in the best light to the next person they talk to.

I strongly recommend participating in the pre-conference panel preparations because from listening in on them, you have access to some questions that may not be asked during the actual session. Having these content based questions at your fingertips is great for networking breaks and cocktail hour conversations because they demonstrate your own informed interest in the topic.

Questions for research

The key to writing engaging panels comes from asking the right questions during research. The specific points in session descriptions rarely match the specific points that speakers actually cover, but more informed and current descriptions are enticing for the higher level speakers you want. When you're reaching out to professionals who attend and speak at a lot of conferences, it is helpful to get their attention with fresh and knowledgeable content.

The classic icebreaker for a research call is, "What is keeping you up at night?" In fact, this is the sentiment most of your questions are trying to find the answer to. They may be up at night because of worry or because of excitement.

"If you actively engage people, they will come to you."

Refer back to your research. "Given that the FDA has made it more difficult to...., how are you going to....?" "I was speaking to someone from another company, and they think x, y, and z will happen. How will that impact your business?" "What new opportunities are you looking at based on new federal investment in.... ?"

Add enough detail and presumptions to give the person you're interviewing an opportunity to disagree with the premise. Disagreements will strengthen your understanding of the topic in general. Being familiar with different approaches and interpretations to a perennial business challenge will make you sound experienced. Understanding the question is more important than knowing the answer because if industry experts are still exploring this question, it means that there is no authoritative answer yet.

Being familiar with key points of disagreement is how you demonstrate that you understand a topic and that you pay attention when others talk.

Basic Research Questions

- What opportunities do you see at this moment?
- What challenges are you facing?
- How have you worked on this problem over the past year?
- How have you prepared for the upcoming year?
- Is there anyone out there who is addressing this issue in a successful way?
- Have any companies come up with any innovative ways to solve this problem?
- What are you looking to accomplish?
- How do you plan to change your process over the coming year?
- What worked in the past that may need to change going forward?

Use questions to fill in the gaps

You should consistently ask for intelligence on competing events. While building Walmart, Sam Walton used to shop at competing stores on a weekly basis to see what his stores could be doing better. It isn't likely that competing event companies will allow you to attend (I've had competitors try to get into my events - trust me, they won't be trying that again!), so asking your contacts questions about those events are your key to gathering competitive intelligence.

I also write constantly. I try to turn all my call notes into readable paragraphs so I can see what may be missing. This informs future questions. Writing is a great exercise to flex your question muscles because you will see where there are holes in your understanding of a topic, or simply areas that you might explore more deeply.

You ought to examine the questions you use on a daily basis - why not?

CHAPTER SIX RESOURCES

Books:

- *How to Win Friends and Influence People*, Dale Carnegie

- *Awaken the Giant Within*, Anthony Robbins

- *Sam Walton: Made in America*, Sam Walton

CHAPTER SIX EXERCISES

What are your top five interview questions for your current or next event?

What are your top five social questions?

During the cocktail hour, ask people about the city where your next event is being held. Write a short blog article based on the answers.

Chapter 7

ENJOY BUILDING RELATIONSHIPS

"You can have everything in life you want, if you will just help other people get what they want." – Zig Ziglar

Did I ever tell you about the time a head of state told me to turn down my music, and I refused? The company I worked for branded itself by playing "Money" by Pink Floyd to introduce each event, and our keynote speaker was a former prime minister of Peru who was now an advisor for a private equity firm. As he made his way onstage for his keynote presentation, he turned to me and asked, "Can we please turn the music down?" I told him I couldn't because this was a standard company procedure. That's right. One of the most powerful men in the Western Hemisphere told me to turn my music down, and I told him no. Take *that*, authority!

You will meet thousands of people over the course of your career as a producer. This is one of the fringe benefits you get from doing it. While your boss might make you pay out of pocket for a hotel movie you watch after running an event that made him a quarter million dollars, the relationships you build on the job are specifically yours. Your job becomes much easier when you develop a genuine relationship with the conference constituents, and it is the most valuable thing you can do.

Sell yourself first

From the moment you begin working on your first event, you have the opportunity to demonstrate your work ethic. Since you're following the advice about how to be a great employee offered in Chapter Two, all the stakeholders in your event are witnessing your punctuality, attention to detail, professional demeanor, and a myriad of other qualities that demonstrate your work ethic. Hundreds of people will be first hand witnesses of your ability to multi-task, explain complex topics, and treat them like your most important customer. You don't ask much of them other than attending your events (which benefits them more than you) so in the future, they are likely to take your calls.

Look for any opportunity to follow through and do a bit more than expected. Always personalize emails. Answer emails quickly – even better, pick up the phone and call.

Be a connector

The best way to benefit anyone is to introduce them to someone who can help them. Fortunately, introducing people is an infinitely sustainable way for you to add value. This is how community and organizational leaders make their impact. Like it or not, you are now a politician. Or at least a connector. Malcolm Gladwell describes Connectors in his book *The Tipping Point*.

> "*Connectors* are the people in a community who know large numbers of people and who are in the habit of making introductions. A connector is essentially the social equivalent of a computer network hub. They usually know people across an array of social, cultural, professional, and economic circles, and make a habit of introducing people who work or live in different circles. They are people who 'link us up with the world... people with a special gift for bringing the world together.'"

Connectors are a conference producer's best friend. Once you get their buy in, they will be able to introduce you to other speakers, audience members, and strategic partners to help grow your event.

Hosting the event – tying things together

The connections people make at one of your events can lead to a billion dollar deal, depending on the industry. You know all of the speakers, and probably some of the guests. And because you've had thorough conversations with them about their projects, business needs, and professional interests, you are in a great position to introduce them to people with similar interests, or solutions to their problems. Since you've collaborated with your sponsorship sales staff, you're also familiar with what expertise the event sponsors have, and you can introduce them to people who might benefit from their services. This is high-end customer service to be sure. But it's also socially gracious to ensure that each of your guests has the most valuable experience that you can provide for them.

Rich Dad/Poor Dad author Robert Kiyosaki suggests the key to success for an entrepreneur is being able to take himself out of business processes as much as possible. He's talking about scalability. You want to do the same at the conference.

"Introducing people is an infinitely sustainable way for you to add value."

Taking yourself out of it may sound like a contradiction to owning the event and being a noticeable host, but it's not. It's just a reminder that even with all of your efforts, the event is ultimately about your guests, not you.

True, you are trying to attract people's attention, but the ultimate goal is to step out of the way before they actually engage, so that they can engage with someone who can help them advance their career. This could be the moderator of the next panel, a vendor who is running an exhibition booth, or a colleague in the audience who they may want to meet.

But before you step out of the way, you do need to engage their attention.

Reach out through all media at your disposal

Keep yourself on top of your game by connecting with everyone you meet doing the course of producing and running the event. You can use LinkedIn, Twitter, and other appropriate social media outlets. Remember: it's your relationship, and this is how you nurture it beyond the parameters of your job.

Using social media to enhance your relationships gives you the opportunity to develop online expertise. Each platform has a protocol for how to be more effective. Social media gurus such as Guy Kawasaki, former Chief Evangelist of Apple, and entrepreneur Gary Vaynerchuk offer books on the topic.

Don't rely on your memory

At an event, you meet hundreds of people, and thousands over the course of a year. You'll only remember a small portion of these. I don't even try. Instead, I maintain a personal Salesforce account where I can track everyone's information and keep notes on our last conversation.

Bill Clinton famously took notes on every single person he met on 3x5 cards and kept it in a cardboard box. According to biographer David Maraniss, Clinton "spent time each night combing through the file, placing telephone calls, and writing notes to friends who might help his campaign." George H. W. Bush was known as the Rolodex Kid, because he kept copious notes about his contacts.

An important lesson can be learned from such master networkers. You can maintain contacts through Microsoft Outlook, but I recommend the full CRM so you can note whatever details you need.

A good habit is to make notes on the back of business cards after you exchange them with new colleagues. Write down a few brief words about what you talked about and use that for a personalized follow up, or for future reference.

Developing and maintaining your network will not only make it easier to produce higher quality events, it will open unforeseen doors for whatever future endeavors come your way. If you maintain it correctly, it is the biggest fringe benefit this job offers. You may even use it to run for President one day.

Enjoy it

I once interviewed for a job with a company that had Francis Ford Coppola (who, like you, is also a producer) as a keynote for a conference on big data. The tie-in was that in order to use data effectively, you need to tell a story, and Coppola is a storyteller. I think this is a stretch, but given that the producer got to attend the meet-and-greet, it's a unique benefit of the job. In 2014, I worked on an event that had no budget for a keynote speaker (as is often the case). A competitive event featured several paid keynotes, including Bill Cosby. Several members of my team fretted about how we could compete with an event that featured one of Americas most beloved comedians. (This was *before*, shall we say, his reputation was tarnished.) As you may imagine, by the end of the year, the fact that we *didn't* have Bill Cosby turned into a selling point!

Enthusiasm for the job will attract like-minded people. If you are there to work hard and have fun, your network will form around you.

CHAPTER SEVEN RESOURCES

Books:

- *Dig Your Well Before You're Thirsty*, Harvey Mackay

- *Jab Jab Jab Right Hook*, Gary Vaynerchuk

- *The Art of Social Media*, Guy Kawasaki

Websites:

- *LinkedIn*

- *Twitter*

- *Salesforce*

Training Courses:

- Dale Carnegie Training www.dalecarnegie.com. Provides both on-line and classroom courses on persuasion, building relationships, and effective communications in a business setting.

CHAPTER SEVEN EXERCISES

List 10 people you can introduce who may be able to help each other. The easiest way to deliver value to people in your network is to introduce them to people who can help them.

David M. Hoffman

Chapter 8

MAKE FRIENDS WHO MOVE THROUGHOUT THE PROFESSIONAL WORLD

"There are places I remember, all my life though some have changed, some forever not for better, some have gone and some remain" – The Beatles, "In My Life"

The conference game has to be the most ephemeral creative industry on the planet. Not only does our product disappear from existence the moment after it is complete, the companies we work for can't be counted on to look the same from one quarter to the next.

Anyone who thinks it's impossible for something to be higher than 100% has never witnessed the turnover at a conference company. While sudden changes and losing work friends can be discouraging, turnover isn't necessarily a bad thing, especially if you're working at a younger company. Most people move on to bigger and better things. Some people just don't belong at the company they're working for.

One guy I worked with got a harassment charge filed against him by the CFO's girlfriend because he had been somewhat pushy in his attempts to befriend her. (note: not taking "no" for an answer is a good approach for sales and speaker outreach, not for flirting with your coworkers. And to be quite honest, I'm not sure how many times the CFO's girlfriend has to tell you "no" before you decide hitting on her is a bad idea.) In all fairness, he was fairly pushy with everybody. For example, the morning he found out the charges had been filed, he would not stop talking to me about it. I listened to him, told him I didn't know how to help him several times, and finally started ignoring him. He didn't like that, so he picked up an empty Poland Springs bottle and threw it at my head! I immediately stood up and walked outside to calm down so I could handle this in a professional manner. By the time I returned to the office, I found out that my colleague had been fired. There was actually quite a long list of complaints against him. Throwing the bottle at my head wasn't one of them. I just want to let this sink in. I once worked with a guy who had so many strikes against him that throwing a bottle at a co-worker didn't even factor in to his getting fired.

So yes, turnover can be a good thing. Not only because it's good for a company to get rid of bad blood. It's also good for people to be proactive about their careers. If that requires moving on, more power to them.

Remain positive

Over the years, I've heard the grievances of many unhappy colleagues. I think people find it easy to share their problems with me because I began my career as a professional social worker.

Of course it's valuable to have someone to commiserate with as you make your way through the battlefield of the workday, but it is critical to recognize the difference between a colleague who is genuinely searching for solutions and someone with a generally negative attitude.

Even if you can effectively screen the problem solvers from the complainers, is good practice to be judicious about engaging in negative talk about your company. Young employees often visualize a workplace utopia that doesn't exist. The mark of a professional is recognizing that the petty things people complain about are simply examples of on-the-job challenges. While it's obvious that you should avoid becoming close with negative people, recognize that solution seekers can be problematic too. If they've decided that the best way to solve their problem is to move on, they may adopt apathetic or destructive attitudes because they have no intention of staying around long enough for the consequences of their passive aggression to materialize.

One important thing to remember about working in a high-turnover environment is that your loyalty should remain at the company you work for. Regardless of the personnel changes going on around you, you need to keep your energy focused on the ship you're on to keep things running smoothly.

More people will remember your attitude than their specific relationship with you. I'd rather be remembered for my upbeat nature - especially in the face of a tumultuous work environment - than being part of a clique that thinks they're too good for the company they work for. Hint: nobody is too good for the place they work. That's why they work there.

Your next mentor

Someone who moves on to another company could be your next mentor. If they're working at another conference company, they may share some trade secrets you're unfamiliar with. I've worked at several companies, and each one has taught me a trick or two about how to build and market a program. You never know what you can learn as you engage with your constantly expanding network.

Often, people move on to become consultants or work for other companies that attend your events. Being on-site becomes more fun when your friends are there attending the conference. And they can help you network and understand the industry with a bit more depth.

Hell, I still occasionally talk shop with the guy who got fired for being pushy. I just avoid meeting him at a bar because I don't want to go anywhere where there are bottles to throw or women to harass.

CHAPTER EIGHT RESOURCES

Organizing Contacts:

- *LinkedIn*
- *Salesforce*

CHAPTER EIGHT EXERCISES

List five ways you can keep in touch with someone who has moved on. What can you do for them? Who can you introduce them to?

David M. Hoffman

PART III

MASTER FOUNDATIONAL BUSINESS SKILLS

As you may have suspected, being a conference producer isn't only about networking, asking questions, and strutting your stuff on a stage. The real crux of the job is hard work. But that hard work is where you derive the most value from the job because you will be able to develop important skill sets.

In Chapter One, we reviewed some advice anyone ought to follow wherever they work. In this section, I'll turn you on to some of the business skills you will learn that are specific to the producer role.

The key to approaching project management, sales, marketing, and copy editing is to look slightly beyond the boundaries of your role. Your colleagues in other departments will be more comfortable working with you if you understand what responsibilities they have beyond their interactions with you. And you will observe that opportunities for career development surround you if you are creative about how you approach the job.

My goal is not to give you instruction in how to do these tasks, just to guide you in a direction where you can seek out more guidance and build out your skill set.

Chapter 9

PROJECT MANAGEMENT

"A leader is best when people barely knows he exists. When his work is done, his aim fulfilled, they will say: we did it ourselves." – Lao Tzu

Producing a new event is like being given a lump of clay. Over the course of the production cycle, it is your job to mold that clay. The clay is every single person who fits the professional and geographic profile of your event. And you're not actually given the clay. You have to go out and find it, and then grasp whatever bits you can - often snatching it right out of the hands of others - and drag it back to your workbench as you put together your program. Then you have to work the mushy wet clay with your hands, racing against the clock, getting clay on your clothes, squinting as it splashes in your eyes, and hoping it doesn't harden into a different shape than everyone is expecting.

And unlike actual clay, which conforms to whatever shape you mold it to, a conference likely involves the handprints of hundreds of people when all is said and done. Some conference audiences number in the thousands. Each of these bits of clay has goals of their own, individual job functions, and perhaps a vision of their role in this process that differs from yours.

Let's face it, producing an event is a mess. It takes finesse and talent to get hundreds of people to where they need to be on the day of the event.

The good news is that a lot of your constituents want the same thing that you want, and if you can uncover their passion, they will give you their best. If you're attuned to what they really want, your event may just come close to satisfying everyone.

Project management is one of the most important skills you bring to your organization. It's your opportunity to quantify the value you deliver to your organization. Producing a conference is a huge undertaking. You're coordinating the actions of hundreds of people, most of whom work outside of your company. Getting it off the ground is hard, and the bigger it gets, the harder it becomes. You can expect lots of friction as you try to give attention to everyone's needs while keeping everything under control. But that makes it more gratifying when it all comes together in the end.

If you're one of twenty producers at a hundred million dollar company, and your programs bring in over seven and a half million dollars, that is outsized value *you* bring to the company. And there is more value beyond the total numbers when it comes to launching a new event or revitalizing an old one.

Project management is a transferable skill

Project management skills are meant to be transferable from industry to industry. I learned the basics when produced my TV show, *Across the Hudson*. The executive producer – that is, the person funding the TV show – was a major real estate developer. He showed me his own project management tools as an example of how he wanted me to produce each episode.

His major tool was a checklist that accounted for every single component of the building process. To demonstrate the complexity involved with building a high-rise, he drew a diagram of all the moving parts that had to come together in order for a building to be built. It was a labyrinthine illustration, including tasks such as acquiring zoning variances, overseeing a larger number of contractors, tracking vendors, working with an architect, building relationships with neighbors, handling budgets, dealing with banks, setting and anticipating deadlines, pre-selling apartments, and much more.

He created a checklist that accounted for all the components that went into putting together an episode. It included things like booking guests, writing scripts and interview questions, running weekly production meetings, reserving locations, coordinating the film crew, making sure each segment was edited to fit into its slot in the hour long show, selling advertising and working with sponsors, updating our website, to name just a few of the tasks. Each show had a celebrity interview, musical guest, nightlife, cooking, lifestyle, and occasional comedy segments. There were several hosts, a director, and a team of cameramen, editors, and other professionals and coordinating all their efforts was critical to the success of each episode.

His background as a real estate developer made it easy for him to create a workable process for putting together an episode of the TV show (neither of us had a background in television). My experience running the operations of *Across the Hudson* made it easy for me to transition to producing events. The lesson here is that the project management involved with producing a conference has areas of overlap with project management as it relates to overseeing a major construction project.

A checklist may seem like a simplistic tool for an experienced professional, but for complicated tasks, they are invaluable. In *The Checklist Manifesto: How to Get Things Right*, author Atul Gawande offers countless examples of how checklists have increased safety standards for hospitals and airlines. "Under conditions of complexity, not only are checklists a help, they are required for success," Gawande says.

You are not responsible for nearly as many moving parts as real estate developers, airline pilots, or surgeons, so a checklist can be a powerful tool in allowing you to turn your back on the minutia and focus on the big picture of developing content and bringing people together.

Build up your project management skills by recognizing that the scope of your responsibilities includes other people's deliverables and understand which skills allow you to coordinate the efforts of many different people.

Treat the project process like a mini-MBA

Make the most of this role by examining how each deliverable comes to be completed along the way, whether you're responsible for it or not. Some conference companies are more transparent than others. If you work in an environment that isn't so open (a likely situation) you can learn to identify gaps in your knowledge and become resourceful about finding needed information.

> **"Make the most of this role by examining how each deliverable comes to be completed along the way."**

One way to identify gaps in your knowledge is to understand the communication structure of your company. Certain communication has been designed for efficiency. Two people who need to share information have a process and tools in place to communicate directly. Unfortunately, in the corporate world, many messages take a convoluted route to get to where they need to go. Opportunity lies in being aware of these inefficient communication processes within your organization because you will be able to anticipate and avoid miscommunications that are built into the system. Understand where deficits exist and account for them when planning your project.

Leadership

Leadership is about motivating and directing others. This means believing in your project, recognizing its strengths and continually using those strengths to build it out further. It means creating a consensus of urgency about your deadlines. It includes providing a model of hard work for the people who work around you. Most importantly, it requires making everyone look good. If you make each member of your team individually shine, your leadership will not go unnoticed.

One of the biggest challenges you may face is when colleagues' incentives might not match your project's deadlines.

> ### You May be Responsible for
>
> - **Cash flow**, as you manage your sponsorship and ticket sales team to generate revenue.
> - **Marketing**, as you work with your designer and webmaster to effectively communicate the value and content of your event to the intended audience.
> - **Logistics**, as you work with your meeting planner to ensure smooth operations on the day of the event.
> - **Workflow management**, as you coordinate your own deliverables with the rest of your team.
>
> And let's not forget
> - **Product**, as you research the marketplace, write the agenda, and do your outreach to secure speakers for the program.

For example, suppose a sponsorship salesperson has a quarterly sales goal of $250,000. If they have multiple projects, they may be inclined to spend their time on the one that is easiest to sell. If yours is a new event, they may put their efforts into other options that promise more immediate results. It's unfortunate, because the struggling event obviously needs more work. But ordinary incentives lead them toward the low hanging fruit.

Working with people who don't report to you directly requires you to massage the relationship. You need to demonstrate empathy and convince them that working with you is easy and effective. If you don't think their other responsibilities are important, they may not share your opinion, so you to need work with their flow as much as possible. Be a help to them, especially when you are asking for additional work or risk.

Using leverage to turn your back

Producing a conference has so many moving parts that it's impossible to keep track of all of them. If you're working with a keynote speaker like Richard Branson or Elon Musk, you're going to be working on their terms. They may require extra attention (even if you've paid over $100,000 for the honor). If you have several high profile entrepreneurs or C-level executives you need to be able to turn your back on your other, lower profile speakers and have faith that they're going to come through.

"It takes finesse and talent to get hundreds of people to where they need to be on the day of the event."

So how can a responsible project manager make sure that everything that needs to happen is happening? One tool is to institute a series of spot checks to identify red flags ahead of time that will tell you where things aren't going smoothly. For example, although ideally you intend to maintain ongoing conversations with each of your speakers throughout the production cycle, we all know that that doesn't always happen.

To make sure you're not losing anyone, keep a checklist of touch points for each speaker. This tells you which speakers have sent deliverables, or at least been in contact with you or other members of the team. If someone has, it's a fairly safe bet you can turn your back on them and expect to see them on game day. On the other hand, if someone has been silent since you first confirmed them to speak, that could be a clue that that individual requires extra attention. Many speakers will ignore many of your requests but still show up on the day of the event. A checklist is a tool to avoid having to follow up with every person continuously. If they respond at key times, you know they're still on board.

The ability to meet deadlines while depending on people who don't directly report to you is an asset. Understanding how different roles fit together in a project and how to leverage other people's expertise translates across industries. Build this skill, and you will be able to manage projects across different industries.

CHAPTER NINE RESOURCES

Books:

- *Getting Things Done*, David Allen

- *7 Habits of Highly Effective People*, Stephen Covey

- *The Checklist Manifesto*, Atul Gawande

Classes and Certifications:

- PMP Certification. Project Management Institute. www.pmi.org

- Udemy Online Project Management Course www.udemy.com/courses/business/project-management

CHAPTER NINE EXERCISES

How many moving parts can you name as a part of the production process?

How can you leverage other stakeholders' goals to ensure that they help your event go smoothly?

Chapter 10

PUT WIND IN YOUR SALES

"A. Always B. Be C. Closing" – Blake, *Glenngary Glen Ross*

Did you know what this job was when you got into it? I didn't. It was definitely mis-represented. I thought I was to be an international relations specialist bringing together high-profile thought leaders for debates and discussion about critical issues facing their industries. The first time I ever heard the term "thought leader" was during the interview for my first producer job. I didn't know what it meant, but it sounded pretty admirable.

I was not walked through the process at all, so all I saw were the first few steps: using desk research and industry interviews to write an engaging agenda, and visions of the conference itself. When I was done with my agenda, I was instructed to find speakers.

"Where?" I asked.

In reply, I was handed a long list of endowment and foundation investment officers and told, "Start calling these guys."

That was when I realized I had signed on to a life of cold calling.

It was disillusioning. I had done phone sales before, and didn't like it. I've watched countless new producers struggle with this aspect of the job. But the truth is, cold outreach and professionally aggressive follow up is a powerful skill to have. Direct outreach experience, along with the sales management skills you pick up by working with your sponsorship and delegate sales team are arguably the most valuable tools a successful producer develops.

Embrace cold calling

Once I got past my cold feet, I began to like the constant outreach. It can be oppressive, but outreach is necessary so you can put together a robust program. Anyone can conceive of an agenda. It's getting buy-in from 40+ speakers that makes it a viable business proposition.

The ability to make a cold call is the first step towards accomplishing many things in life. You know that brilliant idea you had in the shower? (Not that one. That one's embarrassing. I'm talking about the business idea). That idea doesn't become a reality until you reach out to someone who can help make it happen. If you're too nervous to pick up the phone, you'll have no way to get to step one. Getting over nerves grows with practice. And developing the habit of calling back, advancing the call, and developing a pithy pitch will give you the ability to reach for your dreams.

Making a cold call is an art form that will take you far. You may feel your heart start to race at the idea of reaching out to a stranger, but with practice, you will become a smooth operator. The good news is that a producer gets to practice making cold calls hundreds of times a week.

The key to producing a successful event is to view yourself as an extension of your constituents' marketing teams. You are doing live outreach to their client base.

Applying sales to production

Selling is like playing the blues. Easy to learn, impossible to master. You probably already apply many sales principles to your speaker outreach calls. Let's take a look at what best practices you either already use or can integrate into your approach:

> **Sales Strategies to Use in Preparing for the Call**
>
> - Start outreach by calling past customers/speakers, people who have spoken on similar programs, people who fit the speaker profile. These are the most qualified prospects, and the most likely to join your program.
> - Work your network. Referrals and introductions can take you a long way in building out your program.
> - Understand the profile you're talking to and how they interact with others who will be at the event.
> - Set goals and organize your outreach.
> - Know your program - product knowledge.
> - Know the competition - market knowledge.
> - Have a list of questions to find out what the prospect has been working on during the last year.
> - Have a few specific sessions in mind before you begin the conversations about where your prospect may participate.
> - Use tenacity and enthusiasm when approaching the next call.

Sales management

You're not just creating a product and putting it out there for the sales team to pitch. You're leading the sales process by explaining to prospects the goals of the event, incorporating relevant messages into the overall value proposition, and integrating sponsors onto the program. You've done a lot to help bring about that $150,000 multi-event deal your sponsorship manager just closed.

Understanding the sales team, supporting them, and directing them so they sell onto your event is a valuable leadership skill to

bring to the table. Any value driven organization needs leaders who can drive revenue.

> **Sales Strategies to Use During the Call**
>
> - Check in occasionally so you know you're not losing them when you talk for an extended period of time. Better yet, keep them engaged by driving the call with questions.
> - Describe the event in terms of how it benefits the speaker to participate.
> - Overcome objections by asking probing questions to ensure you address the actual problem.
> - Create urgency by creating mini-deadlines such as letting them know their choice of panels will shrink as others sign on.
> - Build rapport - build relationships.
> - Mention similar people who are confirmed to speak or have spoken in the past. This is called "social proof."
> - End every call with a clear understanding of next steps - know what needs to happen in order for them to confirm speaking.

Understand your company's sales process

You may have conflicts in vying for the attention of sponsorship managers who are able to sell on multiple programs, so it is important for you to understand their process and give them the tools they need to make selling onto your program as easy as possible. Your company likely has a system for sales. I recommend learning whatever process that is. Salespeople can be territorial, so if your sales team thinks asking questions about the process is being nosy, you can read up on your own and pay attention to what you are privy to in the office. There are many different systems.

Years ago, I sold direct marketing programs over the phone. Our system was to find a match for MTB: Market, Time, and Budget. Market - who are they trying to reach? Time - when are they prepared to spend money on marketing? and Budget - how much are they planning to spend on marketing? We needed to determine if we were speaking to the decision maker. We needed to identify objections, and respond by asking probing questions to overcome those objections.

Several conference companies I've worked with used a process called SPIN Selling, which stands for Situation, Problem, Implication, and Need-payoff. The system is designed to build value early and circumvent objections related to long term relationships and big ticket items. It works well with large companies with transactions that average over $1 million. (Sponsoring a conference is a phenomenal deal for these companies; don't let them tell you otherwise).

It doesn't really matter what sales method your company uses. The point is to understand that sales is a structured process. As a producer, you're already doing a lot of sales tasks. You have the intimate product and industry knowledge, you do the outreach, you ask questions to understand client needs, and you use various persuasive techniques to get buy in. By learning more about it, you can better assist your sponsorship salesperson, improve your own outreach, and perhaps move into sales as a career.

Sponsorship sales is your partner

Not only is it critical for you to integrate sales techniques into your own outreach, you also want to understand the process so you can effectively work with your sales team. Treat your sponsorship sales team as masters, and they will treat you well.

There is always tension between sponsorship and producers as to whose job is harder. Personally, I think this is an individual question - people work as hard as they want to. Salespeople have the pressure of asking for money, which producers don't. But salespeople also have the advantage of exchanging a clear monetary benefit for the cost of sponsorship - a room full of their target audience, which translates into potential business. While producers don't ask for money, we are asking busy professionals to take several days out of the office plus committing a few hours or days of prep time before the event. I'm always humbled that they find the value in joining our events. Asking them to do so is no less critical than bringing sponsors on board.

I have tremendous respect for salesmen. It may be clichéd to say the ability to close a deal is what separates the men from the boys (not only clichéd, but sexist!), but it is true. Closing a deal is what separates an adult doing business from a narcissist's speculations and games.

"Selling is like playing the blues. Easy to learn, impossible to master."

If your sponsorship sales team is good at what they do, you stand to learn a lot. If they're newbies, you have the opportunity to offer support. You can offer support by: supplying leads, effectively communicating the profiles, value proposition, key sessions, and speakers of the event, and getting on the phone with them to help them describe to prospects where they fit into the program and what value they get from attending. The better you understand the challenges your sponsorship team faces, the easier it will be for you to help them. The better you're able to demonstrate your appreciation for the hard work they're putting in, the more they will appreciate working with you.

If you support your salespeople well, they will love you. For every $150,000 contract they have out there, they want to rest assured that you will treat their clients well. You are the lever that allows them to deliver outsized follow up. And the company will recognize your role in generating revenue for your events.

Tenacity

The bottom line is that phone outreach is tricky and fickle. Some people are nice, some people are jerks. Some people already understand the value of speaking at your event, others need convincing. The fact is that it is a numbers game. The more people you call, the more easy calls you will encounter. That is reason enough to keep up your call volume. Another reason to make a high number of outgoing calls is that practice makes perfect. If you approach each call with maximum enthusiasm and attention to detail regarding your questions, rapport, process, and explanations, you will get better at navigating these calls. At every place I've ever worked, I've had a reputation for high call volume because I know that the next call could be the contact that brings the event to the next level.

You are already doing a good portion of the sales job. If you strengthen this skill, you add tremendous value to your colleagues and company.

CHAPTER TEN RESOURCES

Books:

There are many books on sales, but here are a few to get you started. There are many structural and stylistic guidelines, and it is beneficial to absorb as much as possible and integrate parts of each into your own approach. When you spend the day leaving messages, it's easy to backslide and forget some basic skills, so continuous reminders are beneficial because it will help you perform at your best. These books are also for sales, which is not identical to speaker outreach. My advice is to pick out what works best.

- *SPIN Selling*, Neil Rackham

- *Rainmaking Conversations*, Mick Schultz & John E. Doerr

- *Selling 101*, Zig Ziglar

- *The Art of Closing Any Deal*, James W. Pickens

- *Go Givers Sell More*, Bob Burg & John David Mann

Accessories:

- A voice recorder will allow you to hear your own calls to improve your technique.

CHAPTER TEN EXERCISES

Define the following terms as they apply to sales in general, and specifically how they apply to the producer's role in supporting a sponsorship manager.

Gatekeeper

Qualifying Prospects

Prospect

Suspect

Lead

Customer

Closing

Trial Closing

Objection

Budget

Decision Maker

Feature

Benefit

WIFFM (What's In It For Me?)

SPIN (Situation, Problem, Implication, Need/Payoff)

Advance

Value Proposition

USP (Unique Selling Proposition)

_____
_____
_____
_____

CHAPTER TEN EXERCISES (Continued)

Chapter 11

LEAVE YOUR MARK AS A MARKETER

"An audience is not brought to you or given to you; it's something that you fight for." – Bruce Springsteen

You put a lot of effort into creating this event, and you only have one chance to share it with the world. That means marketing is critical. The audience is itself a key component of the event.

Building an audience is what validates your ideas and brings excitement to the producer role. Like closing a deal, generating an audience proves that you're onto something with your ideas. It's what separates a blowhard from a businessman. Producing a million dollar event is something to be proud of, not just because your profit share pays your Manhattan rent for another month, but because it proves you've effectively communicated a million dollars worth of value for the participants.

I learned the importance of being able to build an audience years ago (before I had even heard of a career as a conference producer) at a New York City area nightclub called Lovesexy, where I produced a weekly live music showcase called *Tender Lips and Rusty Strings*.

The showcase featured area bands who could draw a crowd, but needed a place where they could play original music. My process for finding bands was similar to how we find speakers. I researched area bands who played on similar showcases or were listed on websites such as MP3.com, which was a social media website at the time.

The business proposition was that I kept the cover charge, while the bar owner benefited by having a crowd on a Tuesday night.

Respecting the effort it takes to be in a band, I offered to split half of the cover charge with the performers. All of these bands assured me that they had a fan base and could generate a crowd. I believe some of them sincerely believed that they could. Unfortunately, there is a world of difference between convincing a friend or co-worker to tell you he'll come to your gig, and actually getting them to show up. After a few weeks, I realized that many of them were promising a much bigger crowd than they were able to produce.

So I changed my incentive structure. I still promised them half of the door, however the deal was that I kept 100% of the cover for the first 10 fans. For the second 10, they kept 100%. This was still a 50/50 split, it just required that 20 people show up to see them in order for them to get the full 50%. The incentive worked, and I easily got the headcount up from then on.

I really enjoyed running that showcase, and got to hear some great bands. But it taught me the importance of closing a deal. If you show enough excitement about something, anybody will tell you it's a good idea. The challenge is to get them to put their money where their mouth is. Without the crowd, the showcase would have been unsustainable for the bar, and it wouldn't have continued, so getting confirmed buy-in is critical.

Getting people through the door at an event requires creativity and an eye for results. You need to make sure the speakers and complementary guests you invite show up on the day of your event, because that is the value proposition that your sales team uses to sell tickets and sponsorship.

The ability to build audience by leveraging participants' networks is key to any producer's tool bag. You are also surrounded by other marketing skills to learn every day. They include copywriting, design, market research, data building, and platform marketing.

Become a marketing copywriter

As a producer you're in a good position to segue into a career as a marketing copywriter because you have the ability to build up your portfolio of marketing collateral. In fact, you are in the sweet spot for freelance copywriting.

According to copywriting expert Bob Bly, "Writers who work at advertising agencies are more in the 'mainstream' of advertising than freelancers. Freelancers handle the leftovers: direct mail, radio commercials, trade ads, brochures."

Direct mail and brochures are your forte. If you've been doing this for even a year, you almost certainly have a portfolio of several brochures, save the date postcards, onsite agendas, event websites and email blasts. You may have even helped develop content for a sales prospectus, or advised on messaging for sponsor client outreach. You have a lot of material to work with if you want to put yourself out there as a freelancer. As you build your freelance client network, all sorts of opportunities may turn up.

Tips for Effective Copy

- Use a call to action: "Click here to download the brochure!"
- Write in a conversational manner.
- Use short sentences.
- Write in the active voice.
- Highlight benefits first.

Become a graphic designer

Not only are you in a great position to pick up some freelance work as a copywriter, you are also poised to segue into work as a graphic designer. In your role as a producer, you are in a position to learn the principles of layout and design as you communicate ideas with your designer.

Why not design your own separate brochure as a portfolio piece? There are many courses and books to help you learn the design principles and software. And you have your company's official brochure to use as a benchmark. Many companies that put on conferences outsource, so you can develop these skills as a side hustle.

Understand the "why"

Mastering the basics of copywriting and graphic design will open doors, but the key to success in marketing is understanding how to turn abstract concepts such as "strategy" and "innovation" into concrete images. Anyone can hire a copywriter or designer on fiver.com to crank out a brochure for $5. But a talented marketing professional earns his fee by interpreting the event's main selling points into a visual image.

Most conference companies have a marketing department that is responsible for marketing the event. Yet as a producer, you're already responsible for market research, marketing copywriting, print collateral design, and list development.

The entire value proposition comes from you. You understand the advantages that both the buy and sell sides gain from attending. You're already doing all the brainwork. Why not position yourself as a marketing expert by understanding the nitty-gritty that supports the effort?

Market research

Market research is a critical part of a producer's conference program development. By interviewing potential participants, reading articles, studying competitive events, and understanding sponsor goals, you will refine your understanding of the challenges and opportunities that current market trends offer your target profiles and be able to formulate the conference value proposition, which informs all of your sales and marketing efforts.

List management and data build

Being able to instruct your marketing associate where to acquire their data for list building makes you an asset to your company.

Your expertise lies in clearly identifying and articulating the top level profiles for your event. You should also be able to clearly communicate what benefits they get from attending the event. This information is used in marketing for culling lists for outreach regarding the event. In order to purchase lists, the marketing associate must be able to identify the appropriate profiles.

Both you and your marketing person are responsible for building your data lists. You should be able to build lists as well as—if not better than—your marketing associate. As a producer, you should be aware of competitive events, associations, published directories, and brokered lists that support your event.

Creating a platform

Earlier in this book I wrote that it is difficult to categorize our industry. I'd like to offer an additional description, which is that we create platforms. A platform is an integrative forum designed for collaborative information exchange and networking. The biggest companies today all deliver their value through a platform model.

In his book *The Age of the Platform: How Amazon, Apple, Facebook, and Google Have Redefined Business*, Phil Simon explains that networks benefit tremendously from vibrant ecosystems of partners, developers, users, customers, and communities.

Simon's book focuses on tech companies and their evolving use of technologies, but I'd argue that, by their nature, conferences are platforms as well, so having a knowledge base of platform marketing is essential.

Like Apple, Facebook, Google, and Amazon, our content comes 100% from our users. At a large and dynamic event, our users may take advantage of different mediums for getting their message across or pursuing their goals. A service provider may want to use exhibition space to showcase their capabilities. A consultant may want to be on a panel to demonstrate their expertise. A clinical scientist may want to use our stage to present their latest research findings. Ambitious executives may want to use networking breaks to look for new partners. Research organizations may want to seat drop white papers. Some event organizers will facilitate introductions or on-site meetings. Some use customized social media sites to allow for pre-event contact and follow up. People may live tweet events. There are onsite interviews for different news sources or promotional webcasts. By providing these communication outlets, we help our users deliver value to each other.

Understanding how we are a platform is key in recognizing the value we deliver. As a producer, it is essential that you recognize your own role in delivering this value because you are the one who goes out into the marketplace and finds the participants will add to the overall experience.

You can build out on the platform concept by expanding your efforts in social media, connecting to potential participants and sharing relevant content from your constituents or your own research. Anything you can do to assist your contacts in their efforts to reach each other builds up your value as a connector.

CHAPTER ELEVEN RESOURCES

Books:

- *The Copywriter's Handbook*, Robert W. Bly

- *Ogilvy On Advertising*, David Ogilvy

- *Commonsense Direct Marketing*, Drayton Bird

- *The Age of the Platform: How Amazon, Apple, Facebook, and Google Have Redefined Business*, Phil Simon

Applications for outreach and registration:

- Marketo

- Cvent

- RegOnline

- MailChimp

Useful websites:

- Upwork.com. Put yourself out there as a freelance copywriter.

- Fiverr.com. A freelance marketplace to generate some clips to expand your portfolio.

- iStockphoto.com. To find photos for marketing collateral.

- Canva.com. For basic graphic design projects.

Online Courses:

- Lynda.com

- Udemy.com

- Coursera.com

CHAPTER ELEVEN EXERCISES

Collect a few of your company's email blasts. Rewrite them so they're better.

Design a brochure for your next event.

Collect all the marketing collateral you've produced so far in order to begin your portfolio. Make an effort to fill in any gaps or areas for improvement as you create marketing pieces in the future.

David M. Hoffman

Chapter 12

BONE UP ON YOUR COPY EDITING SKILLS

"Okay, now here's the deal, I'll try to educate ya. Gonna familiarize you with the nomenclature. You'll learn the definitions of nouns and prepositions. Literacy's your mission. And that's why I think it's a good time to learn some grammar" – Weird Al Yankovic, "Word Crimes"

If you are a college graduate, you will get into an argument with your supervisor and colleagues about style. A favorite fight for many is whether or not to use what is known as the Oxford, Harvard, or serial comma. Don't get into this argument. (The correct answer is yes, you're supposed to use it, but that's not important right now). A sophisticated writer knows there is typically disagreement over style, and a high competency worker understands that it is their job to make their boss's life easier, not argue over grammar.

"Become a valuable resource for people who appreciate an extra eye for editing their work."

What this means is that you should run any disagreements about style up the flagpole. Whatever your boss says is the rule. If you're unsure, make your own mini-style guide based on your boss's suggestions. The one rule is that each document should be internally consistent. It is perfectly professional for session headlines to be all capitalized, and equally fine for them to be treated as sentences. Whatever you choose, use the same style throughout the whole document. Ideally it should be the same throughout the company – if you're lucky, your company has a style guide. But, be warned, it may be different between divisions. This is not an argument to get sucked into.

If copyediting is something you enjoy, become familiar with the different style guides out there. There are many, but the most important ones are *The Chicago Manual of Style*, *The Associated Press Stylebook and Briefing on Media Law* and *The New York Times Manual of Style and Usage*. Whatever your boss suggests, it is a good move to understand which style guide supports it. Not only does this add to your copyediting expertise, it makes it easier for you to defend your boss's decisions to colleagues who feel a need to argue about this trivial matter.

If copy editing is something you can do, you become a valuable resource for people who appreciate an extra eye for editing their work for grammatical accuracy. It is a full time job in some industries, and one that can be done on a part-time or freelance basis. Make sure your brochures, emails, and other collateral are perfect, and you'll have an edge.

CHAPTER TWELVE RESOURCES

Books:

- *The Elements of Style*, William Strunk Jr. & E.B. White
- *Chicago Manual of Style*
- *The New York Times Manual of Style and Usage*

CHAPTER TWELVE EXERCISES

Compare brochures for different events to identify stylistic differences. Note different acceptable styles. For example, session titles can come in all caps or be written as sentences.

Note any grammatical errors in this book I should correct for future editions. (I will put your name in the acknowledgements, and give you a reference for future employers!)

Chapter 13

BECOME AN INDUSTRY EXPERT: GO BUY/SELL SIDE

"Andrew Carnegie stated that he, personally, knew nothing about the technical end of the steel business; moreover, he did not particularly care to know anything about it. The specialized knowledge which he required for the manufacture and marketing of steel, he found available through the individual units of his MASTER MIND GROUP," – Napoleon Hill, *Think and Grow Rich*

You have the ability to take a deep dive into any topic your conferences cover. You write the program, talk directly with the speakers, run the pre-conference calls, and, of course, sit in on the event itself. I wouldn't say you are an industry expert, but you are the conduit through which the expertise flows. Industry experts attend our events to remain informed about important developments in their field. The value of the intelligence we bring together is such that many licensing bodies accept attendance at our events for continuing education credits.

Fake it 'til you make it

There is a lot to know in any given industry. A lot. You know what it's like trying to remember all of the characters on *Game of Thrones*? Mastering an industry involves tracking more moving parts than that. I used to wonder why these experts even bothered with us, given that all the knowledge offered in our programs comes from them. The answer is bandwidth.

We are taking work off of their plate by gathering their colleagues in a room to share intelligence. Our value is leveraging industry networks, and then identifying and matching areas of expertise into a coherent narrative that aligns with the business needs of our target audience.

"Our value is leveraging industry networks, and then identifying and matching areas of expertise."

It is critical to know the basics of being an effective producer, but impossible to know the details without being a practitioner. I always relate to Frank Abegnale Jr, who used a minimum amount of knowledge to impersonate an airline pilot, doctor, lawyer, and college professor so successfully that even the people in those fields didn't know he was faking it. He faked his way through being a college professor by staying one chapter ahead of his students. He faked being a doctor by turning questions back on medical residents, making it look like he was creating a teachable moment. If you fake it, you make it.

Leverage your network to create a "Master Mind" group

More important than staying a chapter ahead is your ability to create what Napoleon Hill, author of *Think and Grow Rich*, calls the Master Mind group. The Master Mind group refers to your ability to acquire specialized knowledge by leveraging your network of experts. "Through the assistance of his 'Master Mind' group, Henry Ford had at his command all the specialized knowledge he needed to become one of the wealthiest men in America," Hill wrote. "It was not essential that he have this knowledge in his own mind."

The key to a successful leap into industry isn't about your core knowledge, but how well you leverage the sources of expertise available to you. Your biggest and most useful asset by far is the network of professionals you meet through producing and attending your events. If you're looking for a mentor, there is no better pool of experts. After all, people who enjoy running workshops and leading panel discussions have a proclivity for teaching others.

Adopt signifiers

Listen closely to how your speakers and sponsors speak with you on the phone and absorb their word choices and other linguistic mannerisms. Their word choices are signifiers. They signal to others that they belong to a given profession or management level. They are clues that allow high powered people to recognize each other. It may be subtle, even subconscious. But it is like a secret handshake. Speaking like them helps you in future job interviews, because you give an impression of high competency.

Signifiers show future employers that are one of them. This is not to say that linguistic nuances open doors, but rather that their absence may close doors.

By speaking with these people day in and day out, you have the opportunity to learn their language. And that gives you more options in your future career path. You develop signifiers by constantly talking with your speakers and reading industry news articles.

Keep on the pulse of your industry

You should be following the news trends your audience is interested in. An easy way to find out where they get their news is to ask them. Most industries have trade publications and newsletters that will update you on the field, and give you leads to boot.

The twenty-first century has also brought us online education; much of it free. You can take college and graduate level courses in any topic. It's a great way to learn the fundamentals of any industry, economics, biology, finance, computer science; anything you can imagine. You may not need to know any of this stuff in depth, but learning it will require your brain to focus on the basics and keep them fresh in your mind.

Pursue certifications

However, this doesn't mean you can't also go into the weeds. In fact, I encourage it. If there is one thing I hope you take away from this book, it's the fact that as long as you cover the basics of the job, you can take a deep dive into any area that interests you. I've seen people working in the financial space pursue CFA or CAIA certifications, which signify expertise for investment advisors, during the course of their jobs and leverage that pursuit into new careers.

"You are the conduit through which the expertise flows."

My point is that when choosing which part of your responsibilities to put extra effort into, choose something driven by your own interest.

Being a producer creates a tremendous opportunity. If you aspire to a career elsewhere in the industry, you are in the perfect position to improve your understanding of how things work.

What skills do you bring to the table if you want to go buy or sell side?

Business Skills

Hopefully, this book has highlighted several paths you can take to become a more valuable and effective employee all around, such as:

- A good work ethic
- Organizational and project management skills
- Sales and marketing skills
- Results driven mindset
- Ability to engage the C-suite through cold outreach
- Public speaking ability to host meetings

Industry Knowledge

You learn about trends as the nuts and bolts of putting together a conference program. Building your own Master Mind group makes you valuable by:

- Having an extensive network within in the industry
- Understanding what perennial problems keep them up at night
- Knowing where to look for solutions (consultants, vendors, industry innovators)
- Thoroughly understanding recent trends

CHAPTER THIRTEEN RESOURCES

Books:

- *Catch Me if You Can*, Frank Abagnale, Jr. (Fake it till you make it)

- *Think and Grow Rich*, Napoleon Hill

- Industry books - especially ones written by your speakers

Online education:

- ITunes University

- MIT OpenCoursewear ocw.mit.edu

Certifications:

- Many industries have these at all levels. Find one that matches your experience and use it's test as a guideline to increase your industry expertise.

CHAPTER THIRTEEN EXERCISES

Who are the main companies in your industries?

Check out the LinkedIn profiles and bios of your attendees.
What are some of their earlier positions?

David M. Hoffman

Chapter 14

WORK HARD TO LEARN THE SOFTWARE

"There is nothing quite so useless as doing with great efficiency something that should not be done at all." – Peter Drucker

You may view learning software as an extraneous skill. As a writer, I just want to write, and I'm not interested in the deeper capabilities of Microsoft Word.

But don't underestimate the value of learning software (the deeper capabilities of Microsoft Word allowed me to design the layout for this book.) The reason your company uses it is because most applications have tools that can streamline your process significantly. In fact, when you think about the fact that a lot of our job includes processing and managing information, you'll realize that high tech is the way to go.

It is precisely because learning software is an additional task that you should make the effort. The fact that most people can get by on just knowing the basic minimum functionality of the software they use creates an opportunity to up your commodity.

If you take the time, you should certainly be able to learn a bit beyond the constraints of what you yourself use the program for.

Becoming the person people turn to when they need help with a computer application will only help in the long run.

I once worked for a company that used salesforce.com as their database. When I moved on, I subscribed to the service myself, and now use it to manage all of my contacts. It took a bit of effort to understand how to use the back end to customize it, but now I can bring that skill with me to the next situation where it's needed. I designed Forumplanner.com by myself using a basic WordPress website and free themes. These are good skills to have, especially if you one day want to go out on your own as a freelancer or entrepreneur.

Every application that exists has tutorials in the form of books, YouTube videos, courses, and online forums that answer frequently asked questions. If you seek out the answers you can find them, and if you learn them well, you can make yourself more valuable than Google for your company.

Some applications you may encounter in the conference industry may include:

Office Suite: Word, Excel, and Powerpoint, for word processing, spreadsheets, and presentations. **Prezi** is an online application used for presentations that allows for more seamless real time edits. **Salesforce** and **Infusionsoft** for Customer Relationship Management. **Marketo** is used for lead generation and management. **Mailchimp** is also used for email marketing - free at basic levels, and easy to use. **Survey Monkey** allows you to create surveys and analyze their results. Not only is this a useful tool to compile post-event feedback, it's also an effective pre-conference engagement tool. (There may be other simian-named programs I'm unaware of as well.)

"When you help people, their gratitude defines your reputation."

Cvent and **RegOnline** help manage and organize registrations (and other functions, such as creating an event website, if needed). **Citrix** creates a virtual desktop on external computers for people working remotely. **Concur** is a program for managing expenses.

There are other computer skills that will make your job easier (and make you a more valuable employee). **Back end website maintenance** is useful because most companies require producers to keep the website up to date. This may include **basic HTML** skills. You may also find it useful to learn **basic photo editing** skills so you can effectively communicate specs and resize speaker photos or sponsor logos.

You may also use **audience response systems (ARS)** that allow for real time audience surveys, **internal social media platforms** that allow attendees to set up meetings without sharing personal contact information, or **customized instant messaging clients** for easy communication onsite.

Knowing software applications is very useful within your company, as you will likely have colleagues who need help using them. It is good to be the person people turn to when they need help. When you help people, their gratitude defines your reputation. Knowing software is also an attractive skill set to bring to the job market.

Now get to it, nerd!

CHAPTER FOURTEEN RESOURCES

Books:

- *For Dummies* series has books on all major business software products.

Online education:

- Udemy.com

- Lynda.com

- You Tube tutorials

- Simply Google your question!

CHAPTER FOURTEEN EXERCISES

List all the computer applications you use for work. What are four functions you aren't familiar with? Learn them.

David M. Hoffman

Chapter 15

OVERWHELMED YET? GET USED TO IT AND LEARN TO TAKE CARE OF YOURSELF

"Your mind will answer most questions if you learn to relax and wait for the answer." – William S. Burroughs

When you think this job is overwhelming, remember: every day begins when you wake up, and ends when you go to sleep. This is true of the worst day of your life as well as the best. As long as you take care of yourself, you can handle anything.

My first job out of graduate school at the University of Pennsylvania was working for an agency that was contracted by the City of New York to look after the well-being and safety of foster children. It was my responsibility to give them a better life by investigating the circumstances that led them into custody, and finding solutions so they could return to their families.

I was a highly trained, licensed professional looking after these children, but the job itself was more about wits and guts than education.

In one instance, I was responsible for picking up a six year old

Brooklyn boy from the doctor and taking him to a new foster home. He was not going quietly, and as soon as we got outside, he ran off down the street and around the corner, leaving me holding two large garbage bags with all his stuff. I had no idea what to do, and in that instant, I wanted to quit my job. Then I realized I couldn't. Because quitting at that moment would mean leaving a little boy running around the streets, even if he was more equipped to handle the streets of Bed Stuy than I was. Quitting my job at that moment wouldn't solve either of ours problems.

I dropped the bags, leaving them unattended as I ran after him. I grasped him under my arm and hauled him back to the car, but my heart wasn't in it. I kept wondering what would happen if the wrong person saw me physically dragging a struggling, screaming, African American child. The truth was, I didn't even care about the child at the moment. All I wanted was out of the situation, and there was absolutely no way out. Only forward.

Another time, I had a meeting with a birth mother who lived on the sixteenth floor of a housing project in Bushwick. She wasn't home when I knocked, so I waited in the hallway. After a few minutes, a teenager peeked his head out of the stairwell and demanded to know what I was doing there. Respecting the privacy of my client, I told him it was a private matter.

"This is where I live, and there are no private matters," he informed me, stepping fully into the hallway.

"I have a meeting with the woman who lives here," I said.

At this point a neighbor stepped out of his apartment, sized up the situation, and said to me, "She's not here, so leave."

A teenager and an adult from the projects were not about to get an argument from me. I left.

Yet another time, I parked my car in front of a Brownsville address and went across the street meeting with a schizophrenic birth mother. While I was with her, a major drug bust went down across the street. When I returned to my car, a police officer pulled me over and told me they almost arrested me for parking there.

It's nothing you can't handle

I'm telling you these stories to set up a contrast. Producing a conference may be very stressful, but nobody's life is at stake. It is never important to anything other than your own sense of obligation to do a good job. Hopefully, this is a strong drive, but it is a very positive and growth minded source of pressure. In reality, there is only upside, so if you learn to take care of yourself, there are no problems you won't be able to solve with a little patience, and your health, time and energy are limited resources. Most importantly, of the hundreds of moving parts you're responsible for at work, your self is the only one you have control over. Even though you're going to do your best to avoid fires, you will still face unexpected urgent situations. While you can't control whether or not these happen, you can at least have some control over how prepared you are to handle them.

You only have limited resources to put into any area of your life at a time. That doesn't mean you can't expand your energy, talent, and circle of influence over time, but it does mean that at any moment there is a horizon where you will run out of steam.

It helps to adopt a routine that maintains the essential areas of your life: your physical health, your relationships, your mental acuity, your finances, and your career. Strive to find abundance in all these areas. When maintenance in any of these areas begins to deplete, you need to take resources from another area; hopefully from an area where you are accumulating abundance.

"As long as you take care of yourself, you can handle anything."

Balance is important because if you don't actively maintain any of these areas, they will eventually become a black hole that takes resources away from other areas. But if you do maintain them, a resource surplus will grow. You need to get some exercise. If you don't, your energy level will crash, your stress will grow, you'll become sick, and too distracted to give attention to other areas. Eventually, your lack of energy and illness will take away from your basic job skills, creating another urgent area demanding your attention. So if you need time to get in shape and eat in a healthy manner, you may want to hold off on working late or taking night classes for career improvement. Doing your basic job skills well, and with energy, will eventually bring your career to a higher level than taking night classes at the expense of your health. If you're slacking at work however, but finding time to train for a marathon, you may want to reevaluate in the other direction, reducing the marathon training until you are performing your basic responsibilities are at an appropriate level.

The most basic truth you can understand about getting through the day is this: If you get enough sleep, anything is possible. If you don't, nothing is. You need to manage your energy to be at your sharpest and most productive at all times.

Beyond sleep, you want to make sure you get exercise, eat right, work on a relaxing hobby, attend to your relationships, and keep yourself centered.

Your boss will never tell you to go home because you need sleep. Even if he or she is well meaning, he won't know what is going on with your body or your personal life. If you take care of yourself, you will be able to tackle whatever challenges are created by going home at a reasonable hour instead of burning yourself out. Nobody can help you if you get burned out.

Same goes for exercise. This is not a fitness book. I'm just telling you, make sure you get your heart rate up several times a week. Get up and walk around the office a few times a day - walk over to colleagues' desks instead of calling or sending email. Stretch throughout the day. Do pushups in the morning. Don't let the sedentary life overcome you. Your boss wants you at the desk working. He is not going to coax you to move around, so you need to do it on your own.

Eat correctly. I'm not a nutritionist, but there are some basic guidelines you can follow to understand your body's energy flow. On conference days, I always eat a high protein breakfast (and pay for it myself if the company won't reimburse me) because you need protein to get through the day without crashing. Most continental breakfasts are full of carb heavy foods like croissants and bagels. Loading up on carbs and then trying to get through the day on coffee is a recipe for disaster. Handling on-site problems is hell if your energy is crashing.

You need to trust your subconscious mind to deal with work problems without the added energy drain that comes from worrying. I meditate at least ten minutes every day, but it's more important to take all that energy you've dumped into your job and recharge.

Handle your finances. Pay your bills, manage your savings and investments, call your mother. Don't let your job become a bottomless pit of your time because the only person looking after your overall well-being is you.

CHAPTER FIFTEEN RESOURCES

Books:

- *Wherever you Go, There You Are: Mindfulness Meditation in Everyday Life*, Jon Kabat-Zinn

- *The Four Hour Body*, Tim Ferriss

Online education:

- *Headspace* or *Calm*. For short, guided meditations.

CHAPTER FIFTEEN EXERCISES

Make a list of your values. Remember to take care of yourself first and not let the turmoil of this job overshadow what is important. Some values relate to: Relationships, health, fitness, finances, creative hobbies

Once a week check your values list. Are you attending to your own needs first? Your boss will appreciate you looking after one of his most important assets. (You. It's you. In case that went over your head, one of his most important assets is you.)

David M. Hoffman

PART IV

THE GOOD LIFE

Imagine a well lived life. Would it be filled with interesting and successful people? Would it involve being well travelled and staying in resort hotels? Having an insider's perspective about how the world works? Being at the center of something people want to be a part of?

We both know that's not what this job is all about. Even the hiring manager who oversold the production role to you didn't make it sound that glamorous. The truth is that this job can be a drudge. Repetitive, easy and difficult at the same time. Not to mention thankless. And nobody has heard of this profession. Nobody.

But it's not as bad as all that, either.

I've had some bucket list worthy life experiences while on the clock. The Honda Classic ran concurrently with a hedge fund event I hosted at the PGA resort in Palm Beach Gardens. A sponsored Napa Valley winery tour included a private gallery of original Stanley Mouse prints. Stanley Mouse is the visionary behind some iconic rock and roll album covers and posters. The collection included well known images associated with legendary artists such as Jimi Hendrix, the

Grateful Dead, Steppenwolf, and Journey. Sitting between the CEOs of two major banks while they compare notes about their adventures in yacht racing during an exclusive pre-conference dinner technically made me part of that conversation, which is pretty cool.

Some of my colleagues had it even better.

One had Ozzy Osbourne wander into the room at an event he was running for the pharmaceutical industry in Phiadelphia. Ozzy was staying in the hotel during his tour to promote his book *I am Ozzy* and thought it would be funny to stick his head into a pharmaceutical conference. I've had colleagues live as expatriates in Asia, Africa, South America, and the Middle East for extended periods of time while running conference series. Others have participated in mountaintop softball games in Lake Tahoe and shotgun golf tournaments in Scottsdale. I know producers who have worked with luminary keynotes such as Francis Ford Coppola, David Petraeus, Bob Novak, Naill Ferguson, and Madeline Albright.

It's your choice to focus on what you choose to have on your mind. Yes, this job is often a drudge, but I want you to let go of the tight deadlines, the bottomless demands, and the daily grind. I want you to get excited. About the job. About your life.

You're building your own life and professional story here. Turn on to the possibilities that come across your path.

Whenever you find opportunities to fulfill your sense of experience or feed your ego, take them!

Chapter 16

TRAVEL: IF YOU'RE GOING TO BE THERE, YOU MIGHT AS WELL DO THAT

"I've been to Reno, Chicago, Fargo, Minnesota, Buffalo, Toronto, Winslow, Sarasota, Wichita, Tulsa, Ottawa, Oklahoma, Tampa, Panama, Mattua, LaPaloma, Bangor, Baltimore, Salvador, Amarillo, Tocapillo, Pocotello, Amperdello, I'm a killer. I've been everywhere, man." – Johnny Cash, "I've Been Everywhere"

So maybe I haven't been everywhere. But I remember the day before my first event, the 2006 Police & Fire Pension Fund Summit. It was early summer and I stood with my feet in a slightly choppy Lake Tahoe. There was snow on the caps of the mountains surrounding the lake. I should have been nervous, yet nerves were the farthest thing from my mind as I felt the sand under my toes and the early summer mountain breeze on my face outside of the Lake Tahoe Resort Hotel.

It was a unique view, and a gift. All we're talking about is 20 minutes I managed to squeeze between unpacking in my hotel room and meeting my team outside of the conference room to set up for the conference. But it is also a view that most people never get to see.

Just two years earlier, I had lamented that my job as a newspaper reporter never took me away from northern New Jersey. This was discouraging, because as a writer, I yearned for the romance of seeing different cities. Setting foot in a new location can add a layer of intimacy to your writing by allowing you to connect with people on a deeper level.

Now I was to regularly set foot in different parts of the country as part of my job.

Hold on to the romantic image of travel

If you've already run a few events, you probably have a love-hate relationship with travel. This chapter is meant to help you focus on the love. Keeping in mind your favorite trips—who you were with, what moved you—will diminish some of those negative associations slowly building up in your mind with regard to airplanes, hotels, and luggage.

Business travelers get jaded very quickly. Travel can be a drag. Not only that, but some people I've worked for remind me of the scene in *Swimming with Sharks* where Kevin Spacey throws a binder at his assistant's head and says, "You're happy. I hate that." They don't care one whit whether you get to see the city, and don't like the idea of you treating a business trip like a vacation.

But this is your life, not your boss's. You'll be back in your seat working soon enough. As we'll see in Chapter 14, nobody is going to look out for your well-being but you. If you carve the time out to see the city, you will get more out of the trip.

Put yourself first

The first rule of getting the most out of travel is to take care of yourself. Jet lag can be a bitch, and the best way to cope is to eat healthily and sneak in sleep and exercise when you can. Most hotels have a gym. Get your heart rate up at least once. You may spend hours without the ability to move, standing in the back of the conference room, stuck on a plane, or sitting in an airport. Exercise is a good thing. Eat protein for breakfast and avoid too much coffee. If you load up on carbs in the AM, you will be dragging your ass by the end of the conference. If you overdo the coffee to compensate, you'll pay by not being able to sleep that night.

Making sure you get a chance to move includes walking… which dovetails nicely with making an effort to see the city.

Soak in the city

In the ten years I've been producing events, I've seen several unique cities each of which has a deep history and rich culture. Luxury hotel rooms are a nice perk as well, but if you don't leave the hotel, each event is identical, and the only thing that changes is how long you've been on the plane, and how out of sync your body clock is to the city you're in.

> ### Become a SWAT Team Traveler
>
> It's not your fault if you haven't taken advantage of your travel so far. Travel can be draining. If you reduce the stress of traveling, you can put a little more focus into enjoying the trip.
>
> - Take a look at alternative flights and travel arrangements before you leave. Flights always have problems. It will cause less stress if you have an alternative plan.
> - Call the hotel manager ahead of time. Introduce yourself, tell them you'll be visiting this week, and would like to meet when you get onsite. Go to the pre-con meeting, even if it is optional. Putting a face on yourself will make it easier to work with hotel staff.
> - Join Airbnb, and Uber for when you plan to stay at a location for an extended time period.
> - Sign up for hotel & airline rewards. This is how you get rooms for extra nights.
> - Have a toiletry bag ready to go.

The 2011 European Pharmaceutical Public Relations Summit brought me to Berlin - perhaps the most emotionally affecting trip I've ever taken. A five minute walk from my hotel brought me to a tourist area where a portion of the Berlin Wall was retained for historical reasons. This was an unexpected, powerful moment. In my mind, the overarching menace of the Cold War era I grew up in were juxtaposed with the safest feelings I've ever felt in a European City. I was remembering somber images of soldiers, barbed wire, tanks, rifles, but looking at souvenir carts and friendly, carefree tourists.

To me the city was a triumph of the human spirit. I was on the winning team. The values I grew up with, that I had been taught were threatened in this very location, permeated the city. In the courtyard on the east side of the Brandenburg Gate stood a Starbucks next to the JFK Museum. I was overwhelmed with feelings of freedom, creativity, and standing tall for what's right. I felt blessed that freedom and prosperity had triumphed. And I was bathed in a feeling of gratitude to live in an era when we can travel safely around the world, and that my job was to reach across oceans and country borders to bring people together in a spirit of collaboration – and capitalism!

This was a transcendent feeling of exhilaration - not generally how I feel after an eight hour flight before running a two-day multi-track conference.

"Life is short, and you can't go everywhere, so when you're in a new city, check it out."

Putting the melodrama of an American experiencing Berlin twenty-plus years after the fall of communism aside, this particular trip quickened a habit I'd developed as traveling became a part of my life: visiting museums.

In the matter of hours I scrounged from mornings before room set up, evenings after the event, and before my plane took off, I did a marathon tour of the Bauhaus Museum of Design, The DDR Museum (Museum of Communism), Pergamon Museum, the Neues Museum (which contains the bombed out remains of another museum destroyed in WWII), Jewish Museum, and The Ramones Museum (I'm not a huge fan, but it fed my fist pumping feeling of "'Merica!"). The Berlin Wall itself has a fascinating history and is covered in parts with artistic graffiti.

My wife joined me at the Cavalieri Hotel in Rome where we took a few days after the 2007 World Series of Investment Management & ETFs Forum to see the Pope speak, visit St. Peter's Basilica, Borghese Gallery, the Roman Forum, the Coliseum, the Spanish Steps (where I almost got mugged), the Pantheon, and Circus Maximus (where I should have gone for a jog!)

Without taking any extra time off, I took the earliest available flight to San Francisco for the 2014 Alpha Hedge West conference. That flight (and the three hour time difference) gave me enough time to walk from the Ritz Carlton Hotel to Fisherman's Wharf and Ghirardelli Square. The view of San Francisco Bay alone is worth the trip. Along the way I stopped by the City Lights Bookstore and Beat Museum to soak up a bit of San Francisco culture from the 50s and 60s. It's where I discovered Allen Ginsberg, whose poem "Kaddish" is one of the most powerful things I've ever read.

In Madrid, after launching the 2014 Private Equity Fund Forum for Spanish Real Estate, I viewed Picasso's legendary Guernica at the Reina Sophia Museum, and visited the Royal Palace. I wanted to see a bullfight, but there weren't any when I was there. Unfortunately, I asked a Spanish colleague about it, and he gave me a look of disgust at even considering the idea - I had to take the brunt of disapproval without actually getting to see the bullfight!

I watched lawn bowling at Brits Pub after the 2015 Great Plains Institutional Investor Forum in Minneapolis, jogged up the museum steps like Rocky in Philadelphia after the 2012 Business Development Strategies for Clinical Trials Service Providers, climbed Camelback Mountain after the 2014 Global Indexing & ETFs Conference, and saw Bruce Springsteen in concert in Boston after the 2012 Pharmaceutical Research Collaborations Summit.

My point is not to brag about what I've gotten to see and do (I mean, maybe a little), but rather to point out that many of these opportunities are available to you if you can squeeze in the time. Travel is cumbersome and difficult to do. While places like Berlin and Rome are amazing, I've also been able to use travel to cross cities off the list. I went out drinking in Dublin after the 2007 UK & Irish Pension & Investment Summit, and while it was fun, I'd just as soon do a bar crawl in Hoboken.

On the flip side, I wasn't inspired enough to leave the hotel after launching Private Equity World Brazil in Sao Paulo in 2008, and I've never been back to the country since. I have no idea whether it's worth a dedicated trip or not. Life is short, and you can't go everywhere, so when you're in a new city, check it out.

Make the Most of Quick Excursions

- Read about the city before you go. I like to know the culture behind the city. Every city has a vibe. (This is why I hit bars in Dublin and Museums in Rome.)
- Many cities have discount cards that allow you to see the major sites for one price.
- Talk to concierges, hostels, and tourism boards. They've talked to hundreds of travelers and they will be able to help you make the most of your visit.
- Avoid unnecessary client dinners. Do whatever you've gotta do for work, but on your own time, let the spirit of the city show you the way.
- Don't eat within six blocks of a tourist attraction - it's usually more expensive and of lower quality.
- Take photos, but also make sure you are absorbing the things that can't be experienced in a photo.
- Do some walking through the city - or better yet, go for a jog. You will benefit from the exercise.

CHAPTER SIXTEEN RESOURCES

Books:

- *The Wall Street Journal Guide to Power Travel*, Scott McCartney

- *Concierge Confidential: The Gloves Come Off – and the Secrets Come Out! Tales from the Man Who Serves Millionaires, Moguls, and Madmen*, Michael Fazio & Michael Malice

- Search "Travel Hacks" on amazon.com. There are at least a half dozen books for less than $4 that will guide you through making the most of rewards programs.

- Rick Steves series of travel guides

Language training:

- Duolingo.com. Learn foreign languages for free using a game like format

CHAPTER SIXTEEN EXERCISES

**Make a list of the kinds of sites you like to visit when you travel to use as a handy guide to plan your next trip.
Open up an Uber and AirBNB account.**

David M. Hoffman

Chapter 17

FIND YOUR INSPIRATION

In 2014, I found inspiration while hiking the majestic Camelback Mountain that loomed in the background of the Global Indexing & ETF Conference at the JW Marriott Camelback Resort in Scottsdale.

This was a rather challenging hike, and during the trek, I had several valuable life lessons reinforced. I hope you've heard these before, and more importantly, I hope you find your muse in the landscape surrounding one of your events.

1. Only Rely on People Who Have Skin in the Game

About a quarter of the way up the Echo Canyon Trail, there is a run that is so steep and smooth that you have to hold onto a steel banister in order to scale it. I got about halfway up and started to have serious doubts about my ability to successfully conquer this trail. My colleagues called encouraging words from the top, but I was becoming concerned about holding them back if I got into trouble. What drove me forward was when the people below me told me they thought I could do it. This was a true vote of confidence, rather than the well meaning, but perhaps misguided words of encouragement from above. Why? Because if I slipped and fell, those below me would pay the price, probably worse than I would.

When you come up with a new idea, it's fairly easy to find people to cheer you on. Much harder is finding people to put their money where their mouth is. This is why finding sponsors for a conference early on is critical. Of course the financial support is important, but more important is having a partner with skin in the game. Someone who is willing to share the risks.

2. Always Find a Mentor

About halfway up, I met a white haired gentleman with a beard. Now, I shouldn't have to tell you that when you meet an old man on the mountain, this is a person you ought to listen to. He had seen me leaning forward to grab rocks with my hands for balance. He advised me to stand up straight. "When you lean forward like that, you put a great deal of pressure on your diaphragm and work against yourself." He also advised me not to take steps that extended my leg beyond my knees. I took his advice and had a much easier time.

When working on any new project, the best thing you can do is utilize the wisdom of others – this is the entire premise of attending a conference. From writing the agenda to running the sessions, the quality of a conference program depends on the wisdom of the industry people you rely on for input. While research papers and industry overviews make for insightful sessions, never underestimate the value of panels where practitioners share what they've been working on over the past year. As already mentioned, their skin in the game makes for a valuable perspective.

3. Be Nice to Those You Meet on the Way Up Because You Will Meet Them on the Way Down

I'm such a slow hiker that this one applies more to the people who passed me on their way up and then again on their way down. But it illustrates the community that can form on the mountain. It pays to be friendly, because when you're struggling, some familiar faces are a comfort.

It's a reminder that as you climb the ladder of success, remember who helped get you there. Networking and team building are lifelong processes. While the whole "up" and "down" analogy might not be appropriate, the idea is to remember who is there to help out when you need help and treat them with appreciation.

4. If You Focus on the Next Step, You Will Get to Your Destination

Camelback Mountain is twelve hundred and eighty feet high from the bottom of the trail to the top – about thirty feet higher than the Empire State Building. Within the first five minutes, I almost fell when I stumbled on some loose dirt because I was looking at the mountain above rather than the ground in front of me. Hiking itself can be a very Zen-like experience because each step is a challenge that requires presence and concentration. Yet after three hours of these countless moments I had conquered this formidable mountain.

The biggest scourge of our modern work world is the inclination many of us have to multi-task. Conversely, the biggest challenge is learning how to prioritize in a manner that allows you to do one task at a time in environment where many tasks demand your attention. Sometimes the demands of a big project can seem impossible. But here is the thing. The truth is that you can only do what you can do. So the best approach is to do one thing at a time, and focus on that one thing. That is all you can do. But if you focus, and continue to do one thing after the other, more often than not, you will find out that you will achieve what seemed impossible.

5. Work for Something that You Can't Get Anywhere Else

The view from the top of the mountain is something that you can only see if you put in the hours to make the climb, and you can't share it. Sure, you can take photos, but nothing captures the depth of actually looking out over these unique vistas. And perhaps that's how it's supposed to be – seeing the view from the top of a thirteen hundred foot peak is something that has to be earned. The view is spectacular, and it's open to anybody, but the effort behind the climb makes it something that is experienced by only an elite group of dedicated individuals

One thing I love about being a conference producer is that we get to introduce the event. It's a moment of minor importance – it can cynically be viewed as a way of killing time as the crowd filters in for the opening speaker or panel. But to me, it's a moment to absorb the fruits of my labor. With all the work that my team puts into creating the event (and they do a lot!), it is an honor and pleasure to overlook the vista of people who appreciate our efforts. It might not be "The Ocean" Led Zeppelin sang about, but it is a crowd I helped build.

Chapter 18

CONFERENCE SCHWAG: NEVER BUY ANOTHER PEN

"Why don't I own this?" – Daniel Plainview, *There Will Be Blood*

Admit it. You like free stuff. I mean, what's better than free stuff? (The correct answer would be: expensive stuff. But that's not what we're talking about right now). The opportunity to stock up on some neat schwag is a benefit of being a conference producer. My kids are still young enough that they don't know the difference between a free piece of junk and a bonafide gift. They just know that when Daddy travels, they make out like it's Christmas.

> **"If you want to develop a career in marketing and promotions, you have the opportunity to become an expert in promotional items."**

So grab whatever entices you, and don't stop until you're satisfied. After all, who can't use another pen?

Develop an expertise in promotional items

OK, you may want to show a little discretion when you stock up on pens. The exhibitors are trying to meet the conference attendees, not you.

If you want to develop a career in marketing and promotions, you have the opportunity to become an expert. Being surrounded by promotional items is that it offers you a peak at what is state of the art.

You will become versed in what kinds of promotional items are available; knowledge that will pay off in when you're asked for advice by sponsors or other colleagues looking to display at an event. If you pay attention, you can learn a thing or two about exhibition stands and booths, strategies for manning the booth, and how to best leverage an exhibition room.

Companies offer promotional items for several reasons. First, they want to attract people to their booth. The more enticing the item, the more likely it is that someone will wander by and engage in a conversation.

The second is branding. Your exhibitors want industry folks to think of them whenever you use those items so that they are top of mind when they are making decisions about which service providers to hire.

The third is based on what psychologist Robert Cialdini, in his book *Influence: The Psychology of Persuasion*, calls the reciprocity rule. The reciprocity rule dictates that people are programmed to return favors, no matter how small. This inclination is so strong that Stoic philosopher Lucius Annaeus Seneca wrote an entire book, *On Benefits*, about the best way for a ruler to bestow gifts. On the surface, it's a treatise on generosity, but a closer analysis suggests that this tome is actually about how a ruler can most effectively use gift giving as a technique to control subjects.

Your understanding of promotional items may not help you to rule others, but it will bring you great power – after all, the pen *is* mightier than the sword.

Some of the Schwag I've Gotten Includes

- An mp3 Player
- T-Shirts
- Winter Hats
- Very Nice Pens
- Notebooks (As a writer, pens and notebooks are gold to me)
- Collectable stuffed animals (Wells Fargo horses go for $50 on Ebay, and I have two)
- Stress balls
- A pen with a flashlight in it
- Toiletry bags
- Electrical outlet adaptors
- Portable cell phone chargers
- Acoustic amplifiers for mp3 players
- Legos
- Ear buds
- Thumb drives
- Mouse pads
- A book on investment strategies
- A pen with a radio in it
- Sunglasses
- Baseball hats
- Water bottles
- Laptop cases
- Computer screen cleaners
- A remote control matchbox car
- One of those things you lean your phone on so you can read more easily when you're eating

CHAPTER EIGHTEEN RESOURCES

Books:

- *Influence: The Psychology of Persuasion*, Robert Cialdini

- *On Benefits*, Lucius Annaeus Seneca

Other resources:

- The conference schwag items *are* the other resources

CHAPTER EIGHTEEN EXERCISES

If a colleague or client asked your advice, what would you tell him or her was the best promotional item you've seen?

PART V

JOIN THE 21ST CENTURY STARTUP REVOLUTION

The old order is crumbling. Machines are taking over. Face-to-face contact is being replaced with electronic file sharing, social media, video conferencing, and interactive online courses.

We are the resistance. The last bastion of humanity in a world where real life relationships are being squeezed out of existence by technology.

But we already knew this is a high pressure job.

In reality, I don't know too many events professionals who feel threatened by technology. Video conferencing will never replace human interaction. The energy that comes from sharing physical space with colleagues will never be matched, but technology may enhance meetings by creating opportunities for enhanced interaction.

In fact, there are new technologies that allow producers to do this job from their bedrooms. When I started in 2006, I knew industry veterans who had produced conferences using libraries, physical phone books, and fax machines. Now we can do it with email, a free VoIP, Google, and our own wits.

For every bit of uncertainty you face, every strand of office politics you trip over, and every doubt in your boss's omniscience, remember that the startup revolution is here to stay, and likely to grow. If you invest in yourself first, you will bring the best tools to the fight no matter where you work.

Chapter 19

LEARN THE INTRACACIES OF WORKING FOR A STARTUP

"A startup is a human institution designed to create a new product or service under conditions of extreme uncertainty." – Eric Reis, The Lean Startup

Working for a startup company has been trendy since the turn of the century. It is a skill set all its own. Because of low barriers to entry, and an abundance of self driven, ambitious, and creative souls, there is a good chance that the company you're currently working for is less than ten years old. As a producer each event you launch is a startup, and each conference company is an incubator of sorts for these startups.

Beyond that, the conference industry is filled with hundreds of people who are certain they can run a company better than their boss. And many of them are right! So they go out on their own. It's common for people to underestimate what kind of work goes into building a company. There is rent, legal issues, challenges they haven't faced, and difficult employee situations that were hidden from them before. Building a business isn't easy, and there isn't a template, so if you pay attention amidst all the dysfunction, you can learn valuable lessons for future startup situations.

Often after joining a startup, new employees have a learning curve where they recognize that job functions they used to take for granted are no longer part of the company's structure. It's an eye opener in understanding the intricacy of running any business. The founder of a startup may know everything about his business - except how to manage building maintenance, or payroll and benefits. It's hard to know what's not there until it's missing.

Average employees may complain about what is missing. But you're an exemplary employee, and you see this is an opportunity to contribute something extra to the company, and to learn what people starting their own companies might miss. This is specialized knowledge that could set you up for a senior management position at any startup situation you may encounter in the future.

Common sense

If you're working at a startup, chances are your boss quit his old company because he was frustrated that nobody had any "common sense." Be wary of this phrase. When someone complains that somebody else doesn't have common sense, it means two things. First, it means that they themselves have misread the situation, and second, that they don't communicate to others as clearly as they need to. It has nothing to do with the lack of commonality of someone else's sense.

"If you pay attention amidst all the dysfunction, you can learn valuable lessons for future startup situations."

In a startup, people rely on others to have a lot of common sense, and this is a mistake - it's an assumption. If you spent any time as a child watching Benny Hill reruns, you know that you should never assume... because you make an "ass" out of "u" and "me."

Speaking of Benny Hill, you will often feel like the *Benny Hill* theme should be playing as people run around in circles trying to communicate with each other, and taking action based on what they assume others' "common sense" conclusions will be. The way to cope is to be very clear about what you need. Don't be afraid to ask questions beyond the point of being perceived as an idiot, stand your ground when you know you're right, accept there will occasionally be crossed wires, and proactively manage communication issues.

The founders of a startup company can be out of their depths themselves, creating a competitive and overly political environment beneath them. (A true sign of an overly political environment is when you're told the company isn't driven by politics). People develop big egos. They use narrative bias to explain their success, assuming their own touch is the critical factor in a successful event, rather than a well researched topic. They don't respect the power of a good idea. I'm a believer in tenacity, but I've also seen events that catch fire pretty easily, and those that don't. An event based on a good idea doesn't rely on the style of one particular individual to execute it.

The best ideas are ultimately filtered through a vetting process. Some producers stress test new ideas better than others. The most valuable process you can develop is one that evaluates market interest in new ideas before you allocate resources, such as conducting early feasibility studies or assembling advisory boards. Become familiar with early indicators that support the marketability of an event before you begin allocating time and money to producing it.

Take the opportunity to study your company's processes as you work on your own skills. This will give you a better understanding of startups, entrepreneurship, and new business development. Pay attention to how things work as management institutes changes, not only to results, but to how the people around you react to change. People's attitudes are no less critical than their activities. Think big, because your ability to contribute to your company increases as you are able to critically understand how and why it operates the way it does.

As you navigate the tumultuous world of a young company with its politics and experimental processes you should aspire to develop a sense of empathy towards your boss. To say this more clearly **always**

be on your boss's side. You want to be in sync with your colleagues, but you will more clearly grasp the big picture if you remember that your boss has both a vision, and the same right to make mistakes as you do. If you don't trust your boss enough to steer the ship, well, there is a chapter on that coming up soon.

Some Insights to Gain From a Startup Environment

- Identifying functions of your company that can be outsourced.
- Becoming familiar with what is available for Software as a Service (SAAS).
- Understanding basic accounting, legal, human resources, and operational functions and requirements.
- Navigating loose organizational structures - and learn to effectively communicate to colleagues through the confusion.
- Understanding that nothing happens unless you make it happen. You have to do the outreach, you have to make your own checklists, you have to follow up with everyone.
- Seeking out opportunities to contribute in areas outside your role - a startup environment is for ambitious people.
- Learning to think quickly and roll with the punches as your company stumbles through one policy after another.

CHAPTER NINTEEN RESOURCES

Books:

- *The Hard Thing about Hard Things*, Ben Horowitz

- *The Lean Startup*, Eric Reis

CHAPTER NINTEEN EXERCISES

List several changes you've seen in your company in the last year. How has the company adapted?

_____
_____
_____
_____
_____
_____
_____
_____
_____
_____
_____
_____
_____
_____
_____
_____
_____
_____
_____
_____
_____
_____
_____
_____
_____
_____
_____
_____
_____
_____

Chapter 20

GIVING BACK

"Service to others is the rent you pay for your room here on earth." – Muhammad Ali

When I showed an early outline of this book to one of my former colleagues, she glanced at the table of contents and gave me a quizzical look. "Giving back? The hell are you talking about?" We both laughed, knowing the cold, cold hearts of many of the people we had worked for. I replied, "Well, it's obligatory in a book like this, isn't it?"

But thinking it through, it is not obligatory. (I mean, how can it be obligatory? This is *my* book - don't tell me what to do!) It is, however, within the spirit of this book, which is about finding the spark of enthusiasm about your job. I thought back and realized there are several ways we naturally give back, and I've even witnessed some good hearted people actually create events to give back. Creating an oasis of human connection in the desert of the work-a-day world is an act of benevolence in and of itself.

In 2011 I launched a series of events on trial master files for the pharmaceutical industry, a rather dry, technical topic. Heads of research and compliance from industry leaders like Pfizer, Sanofi, and

Johnson & Johnson gathered to eagerly debate and discuss minutia related to compliance and data management in clinical research.

While some events can be fascinating, I wasn't looking forward to this one much, because, well, compliance and data management is boring. Let's be honest. Yet this event was surprisingly moving. One of the presenting scientists told a story about how she had overheard someone talking at a party about how a life had been saved - by a medicine she had developed. She teared up while telling that story, reminding everyone that while their days were filled with paperwork, the results of their work saved lives. The crowd was obviously touched by her story; a reminder of the impact many of them continuously made on people's lives.

Most of the conference topics I've worked on have been designed to make the world a better place. I've never done an event that had to do with anything frivolous. I've run events on how businesses operate in an environmentally and socially responsible manner. I've designed programs outlining investment strategies that allow employers to pay retirement benefits or foundations to pay for social programs. I've created forums for scientists to refine clinical trials to help develop new medicines. There are a lot of important challenges out there, and people who are motivated in their careers are often motivated to make the world a better place, too.

"Most of the conference topics I've worked on have been designed to make the world a better place."

Your events can bring you closer to some of the most pressing issues in the world today. People attend events like ours because they are looking for kindred spirits; people who recognize their role in the system and want to make improvements. In our world, it's so easy to shelter ourselves from problems, but looking beyond our own lives is a way to find meaning. During the healthcare reform debates of 2011, I ran an event on insurance coverage for medicine, creating a collegial forum for pharmaceutical professionals to have an in-depth conversation about issues that were often derided or trivialized by the media. I know a producer who, inspired by real life experiences, created an event focusing on disability and employment issues. Another colleague created an event to address climate change, bringing corporations with sustainability mandates together with vendors who can help them devise strategies to reduce their carbon emissions. The key to success in this game is having the vision to bring a group of people with specific goals together with a group of people who can help them achieve those goals.

And don't forget your company is a resource for small projects. I've had colleagues collect toys for needy children, raise money for medical research, or offer their office space as a resource to engage people in any number of causes.

There is a lot of room for good to be done. Let's get out there and do it!

CHAPTER TWENTY RESOURCES

You've got to look into your heart for this one.

CHAPTER TWENTY EXERCISES

Who is affected by your conference's constituents? What other kind of organizations are trying to solve these problems?

Chapter 21

START YOUR OWN COMPANY

"Opportunity is missed by most people because it is dressed in overalls and looks like work." – Thomas Edison

You will think about starting your own company for several reasons. Because you work harder than most of your coworkers. Because you could run your company better than your boss. Because your contacts want to work with you. Because you come up with all the new ideas. Because you train all the new hires. Because your boss is an idiot. Because you source all the sponsorship prospects yourself. Because your boss won't expand in a direction where you *know* there is potential. Because your company doesn't have advancement opportunities. Because you don't like the office politics. Because you don't like your commute. Because you don't like wearing a suit. Because you don't like that your co-workers *don't* wear suits.

Why is starting your own company the zeitgeist of the 21st century?

Technology allows us - and changing corporate incentives demand us - to realize initiatives at lower costs, and without gatekeepers. This job takes a lot of hard work, but on some levels it is very easy, and on others, it is very subjective. The boss owns the keys to the kingdom.

While they're working to get rich, they're counting on you to rely on that steady paycheck for financial security, and for you to value their praise as a measure of self worth. (Don't feel bad if you do. I'm raising my hand meekly and saying "guilty" as I write this).

A larger company can afford the luxury of testing multiple events to see which ones catch on, especially if they have a large enough staff that they can operate with excess capacity. I've worked for several companies that heavily rely on a single flagship event or series while cultivating a much larger stable of smaller, thin margin events. These companies can afford to run these low margin events with the hopes that one of them will turn into another cash cow.

That's hard to compete with, but far from impossible. You can still beat them by working smarter. Larger companies have more overhead, cumbersome bureaucracies, and workers who are just there for the paycheck. And more importantly, even if they are a slick machine, they can't be everywhere, which leaves market opportunities for you.

"Larger companies have more overhead, cumbersome bureaucracies, and workers who are just there for the paycheck."

I have a lot of respect for business owners, especially founders (not so much middle managers, but that too is another story). I don't always agree with them - and often don't - but I respect their vision, and more importantly, the challenge they face in trying to corral ten to a hundred people into getting behind whatever process, value system, and corporate style they're trying to develop. I have many strong opinions of my own, but these guys have won my loyalty by being intrepid enough to go for it.

You can do it!

I've personally known dozens of people who started their own independent content-driven events companies in the past ten years. And they've all done it different ways. I know several people who run proprietary events all by themselves - producing, sales, meeting planning, and marketing. I know another who, in five years, built up a $15 million company doing business on two continents that made the Inc 1000 list of the fastest growing companies two years in a row. I know a group of four who sold their company to a major media company for reputed $100 million. I know teams of two that work out of shared workspaces and split administrative duties while they focus on sales and production respectively.

This is a field with a low barrier to entry. Established companies cling to their successful events because they're so easy to replicate. Your conference will face copycat competition. If you're not getting copied, you may be facing a lawsuit from a larger company accusing you of copying them because you did something obvious. In addition to the lawsuits and copycat competition, you are faced with economic uncertainty. When things are going well, companies part with conference money, and allow executives to leave the office far more easily. This can create a false sense of value that allows the bottom to drop out when the marketplace is less generous. As an employee, you can rather easily be let go. But most of the companies themselves tighten their belts and trudge on.

The most compelling models I've seen are the companies that outsource everything: sponsorship, production, delegate sales, marketing, and meeting planning. I'll occasionally contract with such companies because I like the flexibility of working from home and the ability to leave my options open. But more than once I've been told that if I have any ideas for an event, they'd be glad to hire me as a contractor to put it together. I began to wonder if learning how to manage contractors might be a way for producers to own their own events, and reap the back end rewards?

Ideas are everything

On the next page is what I call the "Ideas Pyramid" to describe the reasons why people start their own conference companies. The bottom level is the essence of any successful conference career. If you don't live on hard work, tenacity, and hustle, you're probably better off sticking with your full-time job. But I'm sure you know by now, you're going to have to give it your all and more at a full-time job, too. There is no substitute for hard work. If you feel you have a superior grasp of organizational structure, or conjuring and building out ideas for new events, it may be time to make a break from your current situation and go out on your own.

In *The Lean Startup Method*, Eric Reis suggests that startups exist to learn how to build sustainable businesses. Each step along the way of building an event is a part of this process. In the conference game, having an effective organizational structure matters. Speed and efficiency are king. If you can figure out better ways to create quality events that generate revenue, and your current company is not amenable to (or appreciative of) your ideas, perhaps you want to strike out on your own. I don't advocate directly competing with your current company for ethical reasons - you've used their resources to gain knowledge and connections - but if you can find a similar niche that your company doesn't address, why not? Providing an educational networking forum might just help grow the industry in a way that helps everybody.

Ultimately, the process of producing a conference isn't too complicated. Mastering the process alone isn't too valuable. What is valuable?

Ideas.

The "Ideas Pyramid"

Ideas

Organizational Structure

Hard Work, Tenacity, Hustle

If you've done this long enough, you know some events are easy to produce and sell while others are more difficult. There are hundreds of industries out there, and many of them are ripe for conferences and other platforms that facilitate relationship building and information exchange.

Off the top of my head, just a tiny fraction of what is out there includes: biotech - pharmaceutical research - strategic collaborations - healthcare reform - healthcare delivery systems - insurance – regulatory compliance - big data - marketing- human resources - outsourcing - benefits - process innovation - sharing economy - robotics - energy - oil & gas - alternative energy - financial technology - cryptocurrency - payment systems - national defense - trading technology - health and safety - disaster response - artificial intelligence - nanotechnology - 3D printing - sustainability - climate change - water delivery - agricultural innovation - food distribution systems - education reform - education technology - open innovation - intellectual property - microfinance - emerging economies - crowdfunding - private space travel - real estate - financial market structure - operational due diligence - virtual companies. Those are just a few. I'm sure you can name others you've read about.

Brainstorm good ideas. Find a few that entice you - your job will be more engaging if you are personally interested in the topic - and then put them out there.

Build a laboratory for ideas

You are going to do better in the long run if you find the kind of event that burns like wildfire, and doesn't require surgical outreach skill. Some early clues which indicate a hot topic include how quickly and easily do advisors and speakers come on board? How easy is it to engage potential sponsors about joining the event? Early interest is a useful gauge of how successful an event can be.

On the other hand, if you have an event idea that doesn't catch on easily and early, you may look at the difficulty of creating the event as the value proposition. If you find that programming an event requires a more technical background and deeper research, there is a good chance that you've created a unique event because many competitors may not be willing or able to allocate the resources to pulling it together.

Stress test ideas early and often

The key to reducing risk in producing new conference ideas is to stress test topics before committing resources.

Find people working in the field who are eager to talk to you. If you can't, you're being given a clue that this may be difficult. Maybe that's okay.

Develop a clear buy/sell dynamic. How many people are out there in your industry? How many service providers? Who has what to sell to whom? What kind of conference culture does this industry have?

Research what other events are out there. How much of the competition is direct? How many events are topically on the margin of what you want to do? Is there an opportunity to approach a well covered topic in a different city that hasn't seen it yet?

Reach out to some of the participants at competing events. Are they happy with the event? Is there something they're doing wrong? Do they have good buy/sell ratios? What is the atmosphere of the on-site experience? Is the agenda refreshed year after year? Would they prefer not to have to travel? Would smaller be better? Is there a sub-niche of a larger event?

You've already done a lot of stress testing work. And you haven't spent a dime. Now, turn up the heat a bit.

Pull together an advisory board and write a draft agenda. This allows you to put names onto your event to give it credibility. The right advisory board will be open to you coming back to them with questions. Ask their opinion on good locations for an event. Where is this industry concentrated? Is there a submarket where you may be able to siphon off a section of the market from a larger event?

Conduct a feasibility study. Find out what prospective sponsors are doing to market their products/services, and integrate the problems those products/services are meant to solve into the agenda. Understand what they need to see in order to be able to sponsor.

Begin to recruit speakers based on a city and month. Keep the potential sponsors up to date about who may be involved.

You still haven't spent a dime.

If you build enough of a rapport with potential sponsors, you may be able to secure your first commitment before you need to pay for a hotel. This takes a bit of luck but it's not impossible, if you know how to inspire confidence. Chances are you'll have to provide a down payment for a hotel, but you've already done quite a bit of the work towards demonstrating that the event will succeed. Risk is still low.

If you find yourself consistently conjuring and test ideas to generate value, you may want to ask - what value is your company giving you? Don't assume the answer. They may be giving you plenty. They give you sales, marketing, logistics, and back office support. That's very valuable, and not to be underrated. A steady paycheck is useful too. But if - *if* - you have the ideas, understand how to design an effective organizational structure, and have a little fire in your belly, maybe you too can pledge the entrepreneurial fraternity.

CHAPTER TWENTY-ONE RESOURCES

Books:

- *Abundance*, Peter Diamandis

- *Before you Quit Your Job*, Robert Kiyosaki

- *The E-Myth Revisited*, Michael E. Gerber

- *Peter Thiel*, Zero to One

Website where you can find freelancers:

- Upwork

For basic business process training:

- SCORE www.newyorkcity.score.org. For New York based startups. Check your own state for similar resources.

- Small Business Administration Learning Center www.sba.gov/tools/sba-learning-center/search/training.

CHAPTER TWENTY-ONE EXERCISES

Come up with a dozen industries you'd like to run conferences for. Develop a vision statement for each event listing buy and sell side profiles. List competitive events.

Chapter 22

CONCLUSION

"Train people well enough so they can leave, treat them well enough so they don't want to." – Richard Branson

Well, looks like we're down to the last chapter. I'll try and make this quick, since it's the only thing standing between you and cocktails.

I've always thought that that joke was a little unfair. The people who stay until the last session are sincerely interested in the content of that session. The people who are impatient for cocktail hour probably went down to the hotel bar after the last coffee break. The people who stick around deserve better – at the very least they deserve a better *joke*. After all, they did hear the same joke right before lunch, too.

I hope you've enjoyed this little tour through the conference industry from the producer's point of view. If you're new to the role, I hope you've found some new areas to explore in the spirit of career development. If you've been at this for a while, I hope you've been reminded of the power and potential of the role.

Most importantly, I hope to keep the fire of enthusiasm stoked during the long, crazy, and tiring days that we are so familiar with.

I showed an early version of this manuscript to a colleague who expressed concern that I put to much focus on how to leverage the role into a different career path. I stick by that theme. People take more ownership over what they do when they feel they have a choice. I'm still a producer, and I wrote the book on how to switch careers! As the Richard Branson quote beginning this chapter implies, having mobility doesn't equal the need to move on. Career mobility is a result of efficacy, skill, and initiative – three traits that are likely to make you feel satisfied with your job.

"Nothing makes us more comfortable with a person than having a gut feeling that we can trust them."

The producer role is an important one. Without us, our companies have no product. And what is our product? What value, exactly, do live events bring to the 21st century media landscape?

After all, there are so many tools for business professionals to reach their target audience and get their message across. Instant messages, video conferencing, and social media allow for a dynamic interaction in which physical proximity is completely irrelevant. Sophisticated data analytics flood marketers with more information about prospective customers' behavior than they know what to do with. Online education offers a far deeper dive into a given topic than any 45 minute panel can provide.

But these technologies are all lacking in the human touch, and the value of the human touch can be summed up in one word.

Trust.

Trust is what we bring to the party as events professionals. There are countless subconscious indicators that people rely on when we try to determine who we can trust. Our entire lifetime of experience clues us into what kinds of body language indicate that someone is a trustworthy partner, colleague, or teacher. Ultimately, when faced with choices about multi-million dollar partnerships or major career moves, experienced people rely on a gut feeling to sort through all the information they've gathered. Our subconscious remembers everyone we've dealt with in the past, and it lets us know who is reliable. It knows who sees things the way we do. It tells us whether a stranger is likely to be our kind of person, whatever that may be.

Nothing makes us more comfortable with a person than having a gut feeling that we can trust them. That element of trust is what helps people sleep at night. We begin the production process with phone interviews where we ask our constituents what problems keep them up at night. When the conference finally runs, they meet people who can solve those problems. We make it easier for them to get some sleep. That's trust.

As you move forward in your conference career, remember that your own integrity is where trust comes from in the first place. I hope by reading this book you've found some areas that sincerely speak to your sense of accomplishment. Take some time to explore all of them. See which chapters excite you, and use the lessons there to produce your own success.

I look forward to hearing all about it during cocktail hour!

David M. Hoffman

Appendix

THE PRODUCER CIRRICULUM

Books:

- *Catch Me if You Can*, Frank Abegndale Jr.
- *You Are the Message: Getting What You Want by Being Who You Are*, Roger Ailes
- *Getting Things Done*, David Allen
- *The Rich Employee*, James Altucher
- *Commonsense Direct Marketing*, Drayton Bird
- *The Copywriter's Handbook*, Robert W. Bly
- *The Interviewer's Handbook: A Guerrilla Guide*, John Brady
- *Go Givers Sell More*, Bob Burg & John David Mann
- *The 10X Rule: The Only Difference Between Success and Failure*, Grant Cardone
- *How to Win Friends and Influence People*, Dale Carnegie
- *Influence: The Psychology of Persuasion*, Robert Cialdini
- *The Seven Habits of Highly Effective People*, Stephen Covey
- *Abundance*, Peter Diamandis
- *Mindset*, Carol Dweck
- *Concierge Confidential: The Gloves Come Off – and the Secrets Come Out! Tales from the Man Who Serves Millionaires, Moguls, and*

- *Madmen*, Michael Fazio & Michael Malice
- *The Four Hour Body*, Tim Ferriss
- *The Checklist Manifesto*, Atul Gawande
- *The E-Myth Revisited*, Michael E. Gerber
- *Mastery*, Robert Greene
- *The Art of the Interview: Lessons from a Master of the Craft*, Lawrence Grobel
- *High Output Management*, Andy Grove
- *The Hard Thing about Hard Things*, Ben Horowitz
- *Think and Grow Rich*, Napoleon Hill
- *The Obstacle is the Way*, Ryan Holiday
- *Wherever you Go, There You Are: Mindfulness Meditation in Everyday Life*, Jon Kabat-Zinn
- *The Art of Social Media*, Guy Kawasaki
- *Before you Quit Your Job*, Robert Kiyosaki
- *The Complete Reporter: Fundamentals of News Gathering, Writing, and Editing*, Leiter, Harriss & Johnson
- *Dig Your Well Before You're Thirsty*, Harvey Mackay
- *Swim With the Sharks Without Being Eaten Alive*, Harvey Mackay
- *The Wall Street Journal Guide to Power Travel*, Scott McCartney
- *Power Cues: The Subtle Science of Leading Groups, Persuading Others, and Maximizing Your Personal Impact*, Nick Morgan
- *Speak Without Fear*, Ivy Naistadt
- *Ogilvy On Advertising*, David Ogilvy
- *The New Comedy Writing, Step by Step*, Gene Perret
- *The Art of Closing Any Deal*, James W. Pickens
- *SPIN Selling*, Neil Rackham
- *The Lean Startup*, Eric Reis
- *Business Etiquette: 101 Ways to Conduct Business with Charm & Savvy*, Ann Marie Sabath
- *The Complete Guide to Article Writing*, Naveed Saleh
- *Rainmaking Conversations*, Mick Schultz & John E. Doerr
- *On Benefits*, Lucius Annaeus Seneca
- *The Age of the Platform: How Amazon, Apple, Facebook, and Google Have Redefined Business*, Phil Simon
- *The Elements of Style*, William Strunk Jr. & E.B. White

- *Awaken the Giant Within*, Anthony Robbins
- *Zero to One*, Peter Thiel
- *Jab Jab Jab Right Hook*, Gary Vaynerchuk
- *Sam Walton: Made in America*, Sam Walton
- *Winning*, Jack Welch
- *Selling 101*, Zig Ziglar
- *The Associated Press Stylebook and Briefing on Media Law*
- *Chicago Manual of Style*
- *New York Times Manual of Style and Usage*
- Search "Travel Hacks" on amazon.com. There are at least a half dozen books for less than $4 that will guide you through making the most of rewards programs.
- Rick Steves series of travel guides
- Industry books - especially ones written by your speakers
- *For Dummies* series

Blog "Top 5" Lists:

- LinkedIn Pulse
- Forbes.com
- Inc.com
- businessinsider.com

Online Courses:

- iTunes University
- MIT OpenCourseware
- Udemy
- Corsera
- Lynda.com
- Youtube tutorials
- Poynter Institute. www.poynter.org: Has short classes and mini-certificates to help you develop various reporting and writing skills.
- Writer's Digest University

www.writersonlineworkshops.com
- PMP Certification. Project Management Institute. www.pmi.org
- Dale Carnegie Training www.dalecarnegie.com
- SCORE www.newyorkcity.score.org. For New York based startups. Check your own state for similar resources.
- Small Business Administration Learning Center www.sba.gov/tools/sba-learning-center/search/training.

Blog Platforms:

- Seekingalpha.com
- WordPress.com
- Medium.com

Useful Websites for Outsourcing and Managing Workflow:

- Marketo
- Cvent
- RegOnline
- MailChimp
- Fiver
- Upwork
- iStockphoto
- Canva
- LinkedIn
- Twitter
- Infusionsoft
- Salesforce

Other Resources:

- Duolingo.com. Learn foreign languages for free using a game like format

- *Headspace* or *Calm*. For short, guided meditations.
- *Dilbert* cartoons. Read these for perspective. Work is weird. I guarantee you will see yourself, your boss, and your co-workers in these.
- Toastmasters International.
- Open mic comedy shows in your area.
- A voice recorder will allow you to hear your own calls to improve your technique.

ABOUT THE AUTHOR

David M. Hoffman has produced events across three continents for thousands of investors, innovators, and entrepreneurs. He recently launched the North American institutional real estate division of an Inc. 500 company and is currently spearheading their expansion into Europe. He has been a singer/songwriter, newspaper editor, and social worker. David lives in Westchester, NY with his wife and two children. *Producing Success: A Career Guide for Conference Producers*, is his first book. To get in touch, please visit www.forumplanner.com.

Made in the USA
Middletown, DE
12 December 2017